Mastering ServiceStack

Utilize ServiceStack as a rock-solid foundation for
your distributed system

Andreas Niedermair

BIRMINGHAM - MUMBAI

Mastering ServiceStack

Copyright © 2015 Packt Publishing

First published: October 2015

Production reference: 1211015

Published by Packt Publishing Ltd.
Livery Place
35 Livery Street
Birmingham B3 2PB, UK.

ISBN 978-1-78398-658-3

www.packtpub.com

Credits

Author
Andreas Niedermair

Reviewers
Stephane Belkheraz
Herdy Handoko
Emad Karamad
Dony Perdana
Cory Taylor

Commissioning Editor
Kunal Parikh

Acquisition Editor
Kevin Colaco

Content Development Editor
Zeeyan Pinheiro

Technical Editor
Saurabh Malhotra

Copy Editor
Sneha Singh

Project Coordinator
Suzanne Coutinho

Proofreader
Safis Editing

Indexer
Priya Sane

Production Coordinator
Nitesh Thakur

Cover Work
Nitesh Thakur

About the Author

Andreas Niedermair is a .NET developer who is rooted in the web fraction (and still affiliated with it). He has worked in numerous enterprise environments building leading industry solutions and has also contributed to the open source community. He is always striving for a deeper understanding of technology to stay on the cutting edge.

He contributed to the *ServiceStack 4 Cookbook* as a technical reviewer and has held lectures for non-profit associations.

You can contact Andreas at `http://andreas.niedermair.name`.

I would like to thank my family and friends for their patience and support throughout the creation of this book. A big shout-out to Demis Bellot for making .NET developer's lives less painful. I would also like to thank all the people I have worked with and had (technical) discussions with – you helped me to grow in technical and other matters by pushing me further and giving me support.

About the Reviewers

Stephane Belkheraz is a professional software developer with 16 years of Web development experience, with 8 years in developing and integrating Web and multimedia applications with Web technologies including Flash, ActionScript, Java, PHP, JavaScript, and CSS, and the 8 last years in developing, testing, and architecting exclusive ASP.NET applications with WebForms, MVC, SQL Server, native JavaScript, AngularJS, and all the other open source frameworks around the ASP.NET ecosystem.

He has worked for a lot of companies as an independent consultant and developer during his years in France, Spain, and Belgium before joining Microsoft as Internet Explorer compatibility PFE. Now, he works as a senior software engineer at the MCNEXT Consulting company in Paris.

You can reach him through LinkedIn at: `http://fr.linkedin.com/in/ stefbelkheraz`.

"When I discovered ServiceStack for the first time, I thought finally there is a framework that allows us to optimize web applications in a flexible, testable, and performant manner using the best frameworks for every aspect of web application development. This book will give you some of the best tips to master ServiceStack development."

I would like to thank my parents and sisters for their patient support and love.

Herdy Handoko is a senior engineer at Citadel Technology Solutions, based in Singapore. He has been a ServiceStack enthusiast ever since he discovered the framework back in 2011.

Originally from Indonesia, he migrated to Australia to pursue higher education. He received his bachelor's degree and postgraduate diploma in 2003 and 2004 respectively, from Curtin University of Technology, and his master's degree in 2005 from the University of Western Australia. Prior to relocating to Singapore, he had worked in Perth for 9 years within the engineering and natural resources sectors for global companies such as UGL Limited and Rio Tinto.

Outside of work, he enjoys tinkering with his custom-built PC and taking part in hackathons. He has managed to win a total of five awards from his hackathon participations: one award from mining-focused Unearthed in 2015 and four awards from public sector-focused GovHack in 2014 and 2015.

He considers himself to be a polyglot, having worked on C#, Python, Objective-C, Java, and Scala projects and currently experimenting with the Elixir programming language, which shows great promise.

He is also a gourmand. However, he cycles, runs, swims, plays soccer, and tennis to offset his (sometimes) excessive calorie intake.

Emad Karamad was born in Mashhad, Iran, in 1987. He received an associate degree in computer software from Khayyam Institute of Higher Education, Mashhad, in 2008 and a B.Eng. degree in computer software technology engineering from Sadjad University of Technology, Mashhad, in 2010, respectively. He is currently working as a senior .NET developer at Geeks Ltd.

Prior to this, he has held various positions as a .NET developer, web developer, project manager, iOS developer, network application developer, and billing and charging application developer at different IT companies.

His areas of interest include Web development technologies and programming with big data through a variety of database engines.

I would like to thank my friends Mostafa Fallah, Morteza Iravani, and Siavash Mohseni at GoldNet Engineering Group who helped me while reviewing this book.

Dony Perdana is an enthusiast and full-stack .NET developer from Indonesia. Although he is a junior developer, he has been involved with various banking project solutions for the past 4 years, especially on .NET server-side Web technologies, such as ASP .NET, WCF, and ServiceStack. He is also proficient in frontend Web technologies that include various JavaScript frameworks (JQuery, AngularJS, BackboneJS, KnockoutJS, and ReactJS).

He has developed many applications, including content management system, scheduler-based apps, social media apps, Web service-based applications, and so on.

He strongly believes that design-pattern practices and agile development can tackle any problem and also increase team productivity on software development.

In his spare time, he participates in many learning activities, such as reading books, watching videos, going to conferences and meetings to keep up with the latest technology and methodology of programming. He also helps people on StackOverflow and contributes to open source projects on GitHub repositories.

www.PacktPub.com

Support files, eBooks, discount offers, and more

For support files and downloads related to your book, please visit www.PacktPub.com.

Did you know that Packt offers eBook versions of every book published, with PDF and ePub files available? You can upgrade to the eBook version at www.PacktPub.com and as a print book customer, you are entitled to a discount on the eBook copy. Get in touch with us at service@packtpub.com for more details.

At www.PacktPub.com, you can also read a collection of free technical articles, sign up for a range of free newsletters and receive exclusive discounts and offers on Packt books and eBooks.

https://www2.packtpub.com/books/subscription/packtlib

Do you need instant solutions to your IT questions? PacktLib is Packt's online digital book library. Here, you can search, access, and read Packt's entire library of books.

Why subscribe?

- Fully searchable across every book published by Packt
- Copy and paste, print, and bookmark content
- On demand and accessible via a web browser

Free access for Packt account holders

If you have an account with Packt at www.PacktPub.com, you can use this to access PacktLib today and view 9 entirely free books. Simply use your login credentials for immediate access.

Table of Contents

Preface

Over the last few decades, distributed systems have become a complete solution for the purpose of building applications on a large scale. ServiceStack is a framework for .NET developers, which offers tools ranging from the creation of APIs to accessing data in session, cache, and also the database integration of authentication and authorization, Message Queues, serialization, and much more.

In this book, we will explore the relevant features that build the foundation of a flexible, reliable, scalable, and powerful system. It also gives a deeper understanding of the configurations and patterns to solve the problems faced by a .NET developer while building distributed systems.

What this book covers

Chapter 1, Distributed Systems and How ServiceStack Jumps in, covers ServiceStack's technical basics and layout. It also introduces the design principles of APIs and the problems of distributed systems, which sets the foundation for the next chapters.

Chapter 2, ServiceStack as Your Unique Point of Access, introduces you to the IoC-container Funq and shows you how to access data from a session or cache. Finally, it teaches you how to secure your API.

Chapter 3, Asynchronous Communication between Components, introduces you to the concept of Messaging, which is then put into effect with Message Queue solutions, such as Redis and RabbitMQ. Additionally, push notifications from server to clients is covered by server-sent events (SSE).

Chapter 4, Analyzing and Tuning a Distributed System, teaches you how to add logging and profiling to ease the tracing of issues. Finally, methodologies to minimize the HTTP footprint are also introduced.

Chapter 5, Documentation and Versioning, shows you how to leverage built-in functionality to publish and modify the documentation of your API and introduces you to test clients, such as Swagger and Postman. Finally, the validation of requests is also covered.

Chapter 6, Extending ServiceStack, shows you how to write your own plugins, encapsulate services within them, and intercept requests and responses.

What you need for this book

Most examples will simply require Visual Studio 2013 Community Edition, whereas some code integrates specific softwares with ServiceStack. The following is a list of the software required to run all the examples:

- Visual Studio 2013 Community Edition or better
- Redis 2.8
- RabbitMQ 3.5

Who this book is for

This book is targeted at developers who have already implemented web services with ASMX, WCF, or ServiceStack and want to gain more insight into the possibilities that ServiceStack has to offer to build distributed systems of all scales.

Conventions

In this book, you will find a number of styles of text that distinguish between different kinds of information. Here are some examples of these styles, and an explanation of their meaning.

Code words in text, database table names, folder names, filenames, file extensions, pathnames, dummy URLs, user input, and Twitter handles are shown as follows: "As the NuGet package names often do not match the namespaces within, the NuGet package names are mentioned separately."

A block of code is set as follows:

```
public class Task
{
    public int Id { get; set; }
```

```
      public string Title { get; set; }
      public int UserId { get; set; }
    }
    interface IService
    {
      Task GetTaskById(int id);
      Task[] GetAllTasks();
      Task[] GetTasksById(int[] ids);
      Task[] GetTasksForUserId(int userId);
      Task[] GetTasksByTitle(string title);
      Task[] GetTasksByTitleForUserId(string title, int userId);
    }
```

When we wish to draw your attention to a particular part of a code block, the relevant lines or items are set in bold, as shown:

```
    private KeyValuePair<string, string>? GetCustomAuth(IRequest httpReq)
    {
      var hasCredentials = httpReq.Dto as IHasCredentials;
      if (hasCredentials == null)
      {
        return null;
      }

      var userName = hasCredentials.UserName;
      var password = hasCredentials.Password;

      if (string.IsNullOrWhiteSpace(userName) ||
          string.IsNullOrWhiteSpace(password))
       {
        return null;
        }

      return new KeyValuePair<string, string>(userName, password);
    }
```

Any command-line input or output is written as follows:

`Hello John Doe!`

New terms and **important words** are shown in bold. Words that you see on the screen, in menus or dialog boxes for example, appear in the text like this: "One of the key points of ServiceStack is the Code-First approach."

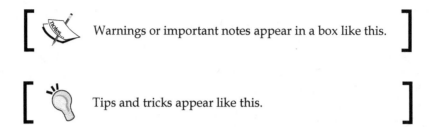

Warnings or important notes appear in a box like this.

Tips and tricks appear like this.

Reader feedback

Feedback from our readers is always welcome. Let us know what you think about this book—what you liked or may have disliked. Reader feedback is important for us to develop titles that you really get the most out of.

To send us general feedback, simply send an e-mail to feedback@packtpub.com, and mention the book title via the subject of your message.

If there is a topic that you have expertise in and you are interested in either writing or contributing to a book, see our author guide on www.packtpub.com/authors.

Customer support

Now that you are the proud owner of a Packt book, we have a number of things to help you to get the most from your purchase.

Downloading the example code

You can download the example code files for all Packt books you have purchased from your account at http://www.packtpub.com. If you purchased this book elsewhere, you can visit http://www.packtpub.com/support and register to have the files e-mailed directly to you.

Errata

Although we have taken every care to ensure the accuracy of our content, mistakes do happen. If you find a mistake in one of our books—maybe a mistake in the text or the code—we would be grateful if you would report this to us. By doing so, you can save other readers from frustration and help us improve subsequent versions of this book. If you find any errata, please report them by visiting http://www.packtpub. com/submit-errata, selecting your book, clicking on the **errata submission form** link, and entering the details of your errata. Once your errata are verified, your submission will be accepted and the errata will be uploaded on our website, or added to any list of existing errata, under the Errata section of that title. Any existing errata can be viewed by selecting your title from http://www.packtpub.com/support.

Piracy

Piracy of copyright material on the Internet is an ongoing problem across all media. At Packt, we take the protection of our copyright and licenses very seriously. If you come across any illegal copies of our works, in any form, on the Internet, please provide us with the location address or website name immediately so that we can pursue a remedy.

Please contact us at copyright@packtpub.com with a link to the suspected pirated material.

We appreciate your help in protecting our authors, and our ability to bring you valuable content.

Questions

You can contact us at questions@packtpub.com if you are having a problem with any aspect of the book, and we will do our best to address it.

1

Distributed Systems and How ServiceStack Jumps in

ServiceStack is a powerful web service framework and it offers many possibilities. ServiceStack's adaptive nature makes the components of the framework fine-grained, which makes it crucial to understand the layout and its components:

- `ServiceStack`: Lets you create your own service endpoint.

- `ServiceStack.Interfaces`: It holds all the base interfaces that are used for the dependency injection-driven internals of ServiceStack. You can fully customize ServiceStack by implementing and registering one of these interfaces.

- `ServiceStack.Text`: In this namespace reside various serialization utilities for JSON, JSV, and CSV. It also offers dynamic JSON processing, diagnostic extensions for printing a formatted dump of an object, URL extensions to deal with the common issues, such as encoding and decoding, stream extensions, and many more.

- `ServiceStack.Client`: It contains the relevant clients to connect and consume JSON, XML, JSV, SOAP, and MQ services.

- `ServiceStack.Caching`: It holds provider-specific endpoints that can be injected as caching storage (InMemory, Redis, Aws, Azure, Memcached, OrmLite …).

- `ServiceStack.OrmLite`: It contains a fast micro-ORM with adapters for popular RDMBS, such as the SQL Server, MySQL, PostgreSQL, SQLite, and many others.

- `ServiceStack.Redis`: It holds .NET's leading client for Redis, an open source and advanced key-value store.

- `ServiceStack.Authentication`: It provides various authentication providers, such as OAuth, OAuth2, OpenID, in combination with its storage providers, such as OrmLite and NHibernate.

- `ServiceStack.Logging`: This includes adapters for many logging frameworks such as Elmah, NLog, Log4Net, and EventLog to provide an interchangeable and loosely coupled logging experience.

- `ServiceStack.Razor`: It lets you add a Razor view engine to your web service to provide a single stack implementation of your service and front-end.

- Various other components, such as extensions to formats (`ServiceStack.MsgPack` and `ServiceStack.Protobuf`), web service client frameworks, such as `ServiceStack.Api.Swagger`, a bundler for web resources (`ServiceStack.Bundler`), a compiler for cross-platform native Desktop applications (`ServiceStack.Gap`), and many others.

 As the `NuGet` package names often do not match the namespaces within, the `NuGet` package names are mentioned separately.

Additionally, ServiceStack offers tools that are focused on simplicity and performance, so (development-) time can be spent on a hassle-free usage. This feature makes it a great alternative to **Windows Communication Framework (WCF)** and others.

 Note that some components are dependency free, such as `ServiceStack.Text` and `ServiceStack.Client`, which do not call for a coupled usage with ServiceStack.

One of the big ideas behind ServiceStack is the Code-First approach. Before you start to design your database, you should focus on the domain design and its **Plain Old CLR Objects (POCOs)**, which then can be used through the components of your stack:

- In Request and Response DTOs

- In client projects by leveraging a shared assembly

- As data models in your database

- As entities in your cache and session

- In serializers and configurations

If you ever find the need to apply ServiceStack to an existing database, it will be trivial to derive your POCOs from the database schema, especially, if you are dealing with a large pre-existing database and coupled usage in the codebase. Therefore, you can use T4 scripts that are bundled with `ServiceStack.OrmLite`, to code-gen your POCOs. You can find these at `https://github.com/ServiceStack/ServiceStack.OrmLite/tree/master/src/T4`.

A message-based service

If you have previously used **Web API** or **Windows Communication Framework (WCF)** you will find yourself in the habit of writing service methods specialized for only one scenario.

A typical interface to search through `Task` instances would be something, like the following:

```
public class Task
{
  public int Id { get; set; }
  public string Title { get; set; }
  public int UserId { get; set; }
}
interface IService
{
  Task GetTaskById(int id);
  Task[] GetAllTasks();
  Task[] GetTasksById(int[] ids);
  Task[] GetTasksForUserId(int userId);
  Task[] GetTasksByTitle(string title);
  Task[] GetTasksByTitleForUserId(string title, int userId);
}
```

There is basically a separate and specialized method for each search option.

In contrast, according to the message pattern, this would be implemented as follows:

```
public class FindTasks : ServiceStack.IReturn<Task[]>
{
  public int[] Ids { get; set; }
  public int[] UserIds { get; set; }
  public string Title { get; set; }
}
```

Additionally, to the basic definition of the message, ServiceStack.
IReturn<T> is already used here. There is no need whatsoever to
implement this interface, but doing so for example gives you the
possibility to deviate from the naming convention of ResponseDTO
class names for the metadata page, and defines the return type on
service clients Send methods.

This combines the various search options into one message, which makes the
following benefits obvious:

- Less distribution of logic

- Less maintenance due to less code duplication in the long run

- Easily add more functionality by introducing new properties in the message
  without adapting to existing usages that gives you a straightforward
  approach to various versions

- Less friction with caching, as the instances can be used to generate a
  cache key

- Easy to serialize and log

- When immutable, it's perfect for concurrency and multithreaded scenarios

To show these benefits in action, let's contrast the implementations, which are by no
means optimized or perfectly well implemented:

```
public class Service : IService
{
  Task[] _tasks = new []
  {
    new Task { Id = 1, Title = "Task 1", UserId = 1 },
    new Task { Id = 2, Title = "Task 2", UserId = 2 },
    new Task { Id = 3, Title = "Task 3", UserId = 3 }
  };

  public Task GetTaskById(int id)
  {
    return this._tasks.FirstOrDefault(arg => arg.Id == id);
  }

  public Task[] GetAllTasks()
  {
   return this._tasks;
  }

  public Task[] GetTasksById(int[] ids)
  {
```

```
    return this._tasks.Where(arg =>
    ids.Contains(arg.Id)).ToArray();
  }

  public Task[] GetTasksForUserId(int[] userIds)
  {
   return this._tasks.Where(arg =>
   userIds.Contains(arg.UserId).ToArray();
  }

  public Task[] GetTasksByTitle(string title)
  {
     return this._tasks.Where(arg =>
     arg.Title.Contains(title)).ToArray();
  }

  public Task[] GetTasksByTitleForUserId(string title, int userId)
  {
     return this._tasks.Where(arg => arg.Title.Contains(title) &&
     arg.UserId == userId).ToArray();
  }
}
```

This basic `Service` class holds an array of `Task` objects that are used in every method for the specific query. Then the matching excerpt of the array is returned.

In a message-based service it would look like:

```
public partial class TaskService : ServiceStack.IService,
  ServiceStack.IAny<FindTasks>
{
  Task[] _tasks = new []
  {
    new Task { Id = 1, Title = "Task 1", UserId = 1 },
    new Task { Id = 2, Title = "Task 2", UserId = 2 },
    new Task { Id = 3, Title = "Task 3", UserId = 3 }
  };

  public object Any(FindTasks request)
  {
    // we could generate a hash of the request and query
    // against a cache
    var tasks = this._tasks.AsQueryable();

    if (request.Ids != null)
    {
      tasks = tasks.Where(arg => request.Ids.Contains(arg.Id));
    }
    if (request.UserIds != null)
    {
```

```
        tasks = tasks.Where(arg =>
        request.UserIds.Contains(arg.UserId));
    }

    if (request.Title != null)
    {
        tasks = tasks.Where(arg => arg.Title.Contains(title));
    }

    // here is room to implement more clauses
    return tasks;
    }
}
```

The implementation of the actual endpoint is straightforward, just apply each filter prior to checking against null and return a matching excerpt.

 The added `ServiceStack.IAny<T>` naturally forces an implementation of the request in the `TaskService` class. You can still add your operation to the service manually, but I strongly advise you to follow the *New API* outline available at `https://github.com/ServiceStack/ServiceStack/wiki/New-API`.

This implementation can be easily connected to the following web page. It once again shows the power of the Code-First approach as it binds to the following interface with ease:

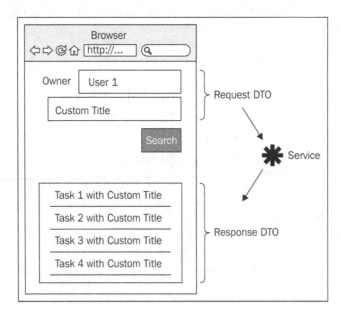

The processing chains of ServiceStack

The ServiceStack services can be hosted in an HTTP and Message Queue context, hence there are two different processing chains, which will be covered in the following two sections.

We will also cover request and response filters and annotations later in the chapter, which allow you to apply late-bound changes to your requests and responses.

HTTP context

The following contexts and their base classes are all derived from `ServiceStack. ServiceStackHost`; they can be used for your HTTP hosted service:

- ASP.NET
    - `ServiceStack.AppHostBase`

- Self-hosted
    - `ServiceStack.AppHostListenerBase` for single-threaded processing
    - `ServiceStack.AppHostListenerPoolBase`, `ServiceStack.AppSelfHostBase` and `ServiceStack. AppHostListenerSmartPoolBase` for multithreaded processing, where the former is utilizing the .NET Thread Pool and the others *Smart Thread Pool* (`https://smartthreadpool.codeplex.com/`) for queuing their work items

The pipeline is the same for every scenario, as shown in the following diagram:

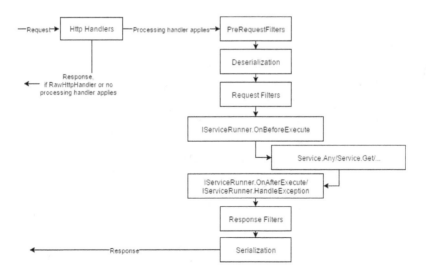

Before any request goes into the ServiceStack pipeline, the functions in your AppHost's `RawHttpHandlers` are executed and the result is in the favor of further processing in ServiceStack if the value is not null. The processing in ServiceStack is done in the following order:

1. The path is checked against existing routes (by attribution and convention). If none is matching, the delegates added to the `CatchAllHandlers` property are used for probing.

2. All the delegates added to the `PreRequestFilters` property are executed, which cannot access the RequestDTO yet though.

3. The content (Query String, Form Data, POST payload ...) is deserialized into the RequestDTO either by default binding or a custom RequestBinder predicate.

4. All delegates added to the `RequestConverters` collection are executed.

5. All the `RequestFilterAttribute` annotations with a `Priority` less than zero are executed.

6. All the delegates added to the `GlobalTypedRequestFilters` property and `GlobalRequestFilters` property are executed.

7. All the `RequestFilterAttribute` annotations with a `Priority` greater than or equal to zero are executed.

8. All delegates added to the `ResponseConverters` collection are executed.

9. Then the registered `ServiceStack.Web.IServiceRunner` object calls `OnBeforeExecute`, your service method, `OnAfterExecute` and `HandleException`.

10. All the `ResponseFilterAttribute` annotations with a `Priority` less than zero are executed.

11. All the delegates added to the `GlobalTypedResponseFilter` property and `GlobalResponseFilters` property are executed.

12. All the `ResponseFilterAttribute` annotations with a `Priority` greater than or equal to zero are executed.

13. Finally `OnEndRequest` and `OnEndRequestCallback` is called and the response is written to the HTTP stream.

Message Queue context

The following MQ server implementations are available (the packages are listed in brackets for easier searching on NuGet) for your ServiceStack service:

- `ServiceStack.RabbitMq.RabbitMqServer` (`ServiceStack.RabbitMq`)
- `ServiceStack.Messaging.Redis.RedisMqServer` (`ServiceStack.Server`)

- `ServiceStack.Messaging.Redis.RedisTransientMessageService` (`ServiceStack.Server`)

- `ServiceStack.Messaging.Rcon.Server` (`ServiceStack.Server`)

- `ServiceStack.Messaging.InMemoryTransientMessageService` (ServiceStack)

 The specific messaging implementations are described in detail in *Chapter 3, Asynchronous Communication between Components.*

In contrast to the processing chain of an HTTP context, the steps in an MQ context are as follows:

1. All delegates added to the `RequestConverters` collection are executed.
2. First all the delegates added to the `GlobalTypedMessageRequestFilters` property and `GlobalMessageRequestFilters` property are executed.
3. Then the registered `ServiceStack.Web.IServiceRunner` object calls `OnBeforeExecute`, your service method, `OnAfterExecute` and `HandleException`.
4. All delegates added to the `ResponseConverters` collection are executed.
5. All the delegates added to the `GlobalTypedMessageResponseFilter` property and `GlobalMessageResponseFilters` property are executed.
6. Finally the response is returned to the MQ.

 Some ServiceStack MQ server classes provide customized hooks to filter requests and responses, giving you specialized possibilities to customize your pipeline.

In contrast to this, you can easily combine an MQ service and an HTTP service and leverage a trimmed-down processing pipeline of the HTTP service. This is possible as one of the core concepts of ServiceStack is the **Message Pattern**, which comes quite handy in this scenario:

```
public class AppHost : ServiceStack.AppSelfHostBase
{
  public AppHost()
    : base ("Ticket Service",
            typeof (TaskService).Assembly)
  { }

  public override void Configure(Funq.Container container)
  {
```

```
    var messageService =
    container.Resolve<ServiceStack.Messaging.IMessageService>();
    messageService.RegisterHandler<FindTasks>
    (this.ServiceController.ExecuteMessage);
    messageService.Start();
  }
}
```

The preceding code relies on the registration of a `ServiceStack.Interfaces.`
`IMessageService` implementation, which gets resolved inside the `Configure` method.
Then all the plumbing is done to register the handlers and start the MQ client.

If you do not want to provide an HTTP endpoint but still use the internals of
ServiceStack such as the powerful IoC-Container, which is an unusual common
use-case, you can use the generic `BasicAppHost` for an extended processing
pipeline such as:

```
var basicAppHost = new
  ServiceStack.Testing.BasicAppHost(typeof(TaskService.Assembly))
{
  ConfigureAppHost = host =>
  {
    var messageService =
    host.Container.Resolve
    <ServiceStack.Interfaces.IMessageService>();
    messageService.RegisterHandler
    <FindTasks>(host.ServiceController.ExecuteMessage);
    messageService.Start();
  }
};
```

This is especially helpful in testing scenarios, where you want to deal with the
endpoints directly.

> The other hook to configure your service is `ConfigureContainer`,
> which is executed after `ConfigureAppHost`. You need to be aware
> of this order when you are trying to resolve any dependency, as
> configuring the container is done afterwards.

Downloading the example code

You can download the example code files for all Packt books you have
purchased from your account at http://www.packtpub.com. If you
purchased this book elsewhere, you can visit http://www.packtpub.
com/support and register to have the files e-mailed directly to you.

A brief history of distributed systems

In the beginning of software architecture there were monolithic systems, they had data access codes and business logic combined in the user-interface code. There was no possibility for modularity to exchange layers (for example when the DBMS changes) or the option to reuse components in other applications.

The first change to this architecture was the introduction of layers, specialized on certain concerns of the design. It brought many benefits, such as exchangeability and testability of layers. The execution and deployment is still bound to a single logical executable thought; hence, it can still be called a monolithic kind.

The next adaption to this design was to add interoperability; with the introduction of a public API external process have the possibility to communicate with the application. This can be done by providing a proprietary or customized message format through protocols, such as .NET Remoting, WCF, sockets, and many others.

Nowadays, the trend of designing applications as a suite of fine-grained services is called **microservices**, which is based on the main idea to orchestrate a bigger system with single-responsibility services. This idea has become more or less standard in the design of Enterprise Applications over the last decade.

The technologies used in the single services are independent, providing the possibility for specialized teams and segregation of internal dependencies. For example, the clients of a data service do not need any information on the actual DBMS, neither do they have a dependency on the used database-specific framework such as **NHibernate**. The design problems of a single application can be solved in microservices by scaling the services with high demand, which also brings reliability, and then deploying them in a version affine manner to not break usages. This approach also gives you the opportunity to use the tools that fit the concern of the service in the best way, whether it be the programming language or the machine they are running on.

The design principles of an API

With all this "uncontrolled growth" of services, managed by potentially different teams with different tools with different "thinkings", comes the need for a unified style or a set of the base design guidelines of the internal and external APIs. There are many resources available regarding this issue, I will cover the most important thoughts, which are discussed further in this chapter.

Usage convenience

Usually, you are defining an interface for an end user with limited technological knowledge. With services, the audience are programmers, which gives you a technical affine counterpart who may come up with every little flaw in your design. One of the main goals in the design process is to keep it simple, frictionless and understandable to the absolute maximum. Verify the simplicity of the design by letting new people try your API, gather feedback and make the usage a straightforward scenario. Also, avoid the introduction of additional dependencies and unnatural bindings to use your service.

Following a message based communication gives you a top-notch and solid base for solving the design process.

Documentation

This may only apply to external APIs, but should also be considered for internal ones. Provide example requests and responses, as well as documentation of the DTOs. ServiceStack provides a metadata page to document the requests and responses that also serves as the base for **Swagger**. You can also add documentation and example code to the operations with Razor views, which is covered in *Chapter 5, Documentation and Versioning*.

Consistency

Keep old versions of your API as long as they are needed to ensure that there is no break in the usages. Be consistent with the naming of properties (also take naming practices of the technologies used by clients into account), endpoints, and formats and ultimately push a changelog to ease migration of changes.

The usage of versions is covered in *Chapter 5, Documentation and Versioning*.

Robustness

One of the main benefits of using ServiceStack for your service is that you can deal with various input and output formats: You can use QueryString, POST-payload, form-data and even extend this by adding your own format for inputting data. ServiceStack also bundles different output formats and can be enhanced with customized content types.

The format binding is done according to either the value of the `Content-Type` HTTP header or query string overrides. If you want to implement your own format, you can do so by implementing your own format:

```
public override void Configure(Container container)
{
  this.ContentTypes.Register("application/X-myformat",
    (req, response, stream) =>
    {
      // TODO add your serialization logic
    },
    (type, stream) =>
    {
      // TODO add your deserialization logic
    });
}
```

Attach validation to your requests as well to provide comprehensible reasons for a failed communication, which is covered in *Chapter 5, Documentation and Versioning*.

Authentication, authorization, and security

Before any other point on the checklist, there's the encryption of the transport layer with the incorporation of SSL for external services.

Processing a request should always capture the following aspects:

- Validate the input
- Authenticate the consumer
- Check authorization to the operation
- Check authorization to the resource of the operation

Authentication can also serve as a base to limit resources for a consumer as well as a common starting point to troubleshoot issues.

ServiceStack also provides several ways to implement authentication and authorization to your service with various providers, which is covered in *Chapter 2, ServiceStack as Your Unique Point of Access*.

For further information on a lovable API design please read
Web API Design – Crafting Interfaces that Developers Love by Brian
Mulloy, which can be downloaded at http://apigee.com/
about/resources/ebooks/web-api-design.

Problems with distributed systems

The design approach of distributed systems is by no means a silver-bullet and
introduces new problems or magnifies existing ones. I am going to discuss some
higher level problems and leave out the low level issues, such as transportation
issues (package loss, network latency), to focus on the stack of a typical
software engineer.

Complexity in design

As such systems consist of many endpoints, we have new challenges to worry about.

A broader set of skills

Bringing a distributed system to life requires extensive skills within the development
team, as well as the operational team. Adding new dependencies to single services
also needs a distributed understanding of the components involved, to keep the
system vital and to be able to respond to requests in a reasonable time.

Testing

Before you ship a system it needs to be tested. Testing does not stop with a single
service, but is done for the complete environment, which becomes challenging when
you need to ensure the consistency of the environment for manual and automated
testing. Differences between staging systems and live systems, such as different
framework versions, can also be a problem.

A pragmatic approach in the long run is to incorporate monitoring to easily spot
anomalies in the flow of operations, as bugs can have amplified repercussions on
the system.

Rollout

The rollout of such a dynamic environment should be done by a fully automated
deployment process, leaving as little room as possible for manual faults.

Operating overhead

Splitting a monolith into multiple processes may start with a certain number of service instances. When applying a failover protection or load balancing and messaging, it becomes a really challenging task to keep such a system running, as the number of instances can easily increase.

Tracing

In a distributed system, one can not simply solve an issue by inspecting a process. You will have multiple places for log files that need a correlative identifier to track down a request and its problems.

There are many solutions out there to help you to manage and centralize logging.

Contracts

To ensure valid communication between two services, you need a contract for a message format and a basic understanding of it. Any one-sided change to this contract will result in a break, therefore we need a coordinated way of releasing it.

A basic solution to this problem is the introduction of versions to the messages, which is basically a method to introduce backward compatibility to the system. As we all know, business sometimes calls for partial rollouts that render components out of sync and "versions" are no longer the magic bullet in such a case.

Issues at runtime

We might come across many issues while running our system that we need to learn from their huddles and perfect our system. Here are some of the problems we might face:

(Un)atomicity of operations

An operation in a distributed system is by no means guaranteed to be atomic, as it might be split into several subtasks that can be executed in parallel or sequentially across service borders.

This calls for a certain mechanism of distributed transactions, to revoke preceding actions when an essential subtask failed. This can also be achieved by queuing entities in a staged pool and releasing them to the live system when all the operations are successfully applied, or otherwise invalidate the changes.

A shared register

When multiple components share the same entity, such as credentials, there is a need to synchronize the register to have the same data available in multiple processes and to minimize hard faults, which fall back to a common database. Another issue originates in the asynchronous behavior of such systems, making it vulnerable to lost updates, which happens when component *A* and component *B* are updating the same entity.

If the components do not have a shared register but rather solve this issue by implementing synchronization, there is a need to introduce a notification upon changes.

Performance

Besides the performance of a single service, there's a natural overhead in the communication when you have to marshal the request and response instead of just working on a reference in the same process.

It is important to not base this process on blindfolded guessing when trying to resolve a bottleneck, which is wrong most of the time. It's better to base it on investigation even if it is hard to apply in a distributed system.

Methods for inspecting performance is covered in *Chapter 4, Analyzing and Tuning a Distributed System*.

Summary

In this chapter the available components of ServiceStack were introduced, to give a crisp overview of the framework itself. In addition to this, we are now familiar with the basic concepts of ServiceStack, such as Code-First and the message pattern. We dove a little bit deeper into the processing chain and explored multiple hooks for injections. Finally, we spoke about design principles of an API and uncovered the problems with distributed systems.

In the next chapter we will introduce dependency injection, which lays the base for a hands-on scenario. Furthermore, we will cover sessions and caching, and add authentication and authorization to our working demo.

2
ServiceStack as Your Unique Point of Access

An incorporation of ServiceStack that takes advantage of all its features, must be made in your design. This integration can be more challenging in an existing application, where you apply ServiceStack at the top as an additional layer.

One common scenario is adding an API over HTTP to an existing system, in order to provide an abstracted and defined public access to internal functionalities. The next step in most scenarios is to add authentication and authorization, and a session storage.

Before we introduce an example application as our working item, we will discuss the IoC container **Funq** that comes shipped with ServiceStack to lay a solid foundation for our design.

We will cover the following topics in this chapter:

- The IoC container
- Session
- Cache
- Authentication providers

The IoC container

Many books and articles have been written on **Inversion of Control (IoC)** and dependency injection, this minimizes the need for an introduction to these paradigms. In short, it's one of the **SOLID** principals that talk about how to loosely couple concrete implementations with clients, for example to exchange implementations without needing to modify the clients.

Funq was made the default ServiceStack implementation due to its excellent performance and memory characteristics, as well as the basic and clean API. It's enhanced with expression-based auto-wiring and lifetime scopes. Nevertheless, ServiceStack supports the usage of other IoC containers, which we will cover later in this chapter.

The central access point for dependency registrations is the `Container` property of your host, which you should only access from within the `Configure` method to register mappings, as this is guaranteed to make your registration calls thread safe.

Registering dependencies

There are two ways to register dependencies. They are as follows:

1. **Auto wired registrations**: The container will resolve an implementation by injecting dependencies into the constructor with the most arguments and public properties:

    ```
    public interface IFoo{}

    public class Foo : IFoo
    {
      // If type Bar is registered, it gets injected
      public Bar Bar { get; set; }
    }

    public class Bar {}


    container.RegisterAutoWired<Foo>();
    container.RegisterAutoWiredAs<Foo, IFoo>();
    container.RegisterAutoWiredType(typeof(Foo));
    container.RegisterAutoWiredType(typeof(Foo), typeof(IFoo));
    container.RegisterAutoWiredTypes(new[] { typeof(Foo),
      typeof(Foobar) });
    ```

2. **Custom registration**: The container will use the provided delegate to resolve an instance, which gives you the opportunity to customize the resolving process and to select a specific constructor.

    ```
    container.Register(new Foo());
    container.Register(arg => new Foo());
    container.Register(arg => new Foo(arg.Resolve<Foobar>()));
    ```

The bundled container does not come with a built-in assembly scanning based on conventions. However, it can be implemented with a few lines of code, as shown in the following example:

One simple approach is to introduce a marker interface and scan for implementing classes.

```
public interface IShouldBeCaputerdByScan { }
public interface IFoo : IShouldBeCaputerdByScan{}
public sealed class Foo : IFoo {}


public override void Configure(Funq.Container
container)
{
  var assembly = /* get the assembly, which should be
  scanned */;
  var types = assembly.GetTypes()
                    .Where(type => type.IsClass)
                    .Where(type =>
                    type.GetInterfaces().
                    Contains(typeof
                    (IShouldBeCaputerdByScan)));

foreach (var type in types)
    {
    var className = type.Name;
    var interfaceName = string.Concat("I", className);
    var interfaceType = type.
    GetInterface(interfaceName);
    container.RegisterAutoWiredType(type,
    interfaceType);
    }
}
```

Resolving dependencies

One principal of IoC is not to pass the container to components and to let the component resolve instances – Components should rather be constructed by the container, which also does the injection of needed instances.

However, you may need to resolve dependencies for custom registrations, which `Funq` offers with the following methods:

1. `Resolve<TService>()` and `Resolve<TService, TArg1, ...,`
    `TArg4>(TArg1 arg1, ..., TArg4 arg4)` will resolve an instance and
    requires a registration of `TService`.

2. In contrast, `TryResolve<TService>()` and `TryResolve<TService,`
    `TArg1, ..., TArg4>(TArg1 arg1, ..., TArg4 arg4)` do not require
    a registration and will return `default(TService)` when a registration
    is missing.

3. `ResolveLazy<TService>()` and `ResolveLazy<TService, TArg1, ...,`
    `TArg4>()` returns a delegate you can invoke to resolve an instance. If the
    registration is missing, an exception is immediately thrown.

4. `ReverseLazyResolve<TService>()` and `ReverseLazyResolve<TArg1,`
    `..., TArg3, TService>()` also returns a predicate for deferred resolving,
    but the overload with arguments will return `default(TService)` if a
    registration is missing.

Lifetime of objects

One of the enhancements applied to Funq is the introduction of lifetime scopes
of an object. By default, the objects exist as singletons and therefore the same
instance is injected into all resolved objects. This can be changed by utilizing one
of the following scopes:

1. `Funq.ReuseScope.Container`: Instances are resolved once per AppDomain
    lifetime, which usually equals the application's lifetime.

2. `Funq.ReuseScope.Hierarchy` (equivalent to `Funq.ReuseScope.Default`):
    It's similar to `Funq.ReuseScope.Container` but the instances are reused
    within the container hierarchy.

3. `Funq.ReuseScope.None`: A new instance is constructed upon every
    resolving.

4. `Funq.ReuseScope.Request`: The lifetime of an instance is is bound to a
    request.

The default lifetime scope can be set by changing the `DefaultReuse` property
of the container.

Disposal of objects

Instances are removed from the container at some point of time and to control the disposal of instances, Funq offers an injection of owner scopes for instances:

1. `Funq.Owner.Container`: When the container is disposed, the `Dispose` method of the instance is also called.

2. `Funq.Owner.External` and `Funq.Owner.Default`: The disposal has to be done outside the scope of the container.

The default owner scope can be set by changing the `DefaultOwner` property of the container.

 The `DefaultReuse` and `DefaultOwner` properties only apply to auto-wired and factory registrations. This is due to the frailty of custom registrations where `ReuseScope.Hierarchy` and `Owner.External` are used.

Initialization of instances

Some dependencies may need a certain initialization that can be done by using a delegate with the signature `(Funq.Container, TService)` as the parameter of the `InitializedBy` method. A good example will be to ensure database schema for a repository, as shown:

```
public class FooRepository
{
  public void Initialize()
  {
    // ensuring tables here
  }
}

public override void Configure(Funq.Container container)
{
  container.RegisterAutoWired<FooRepository>()
          .InitializedBy((c, instance) => instance.Initialize());
}
```

Custom IoC frameworks

ServiceStack offers a simple abstraction layer for the usage of the most common IoC containers. It involves the creation of a wrapper, which implements the `ServiceStack.Configuration.IContainerAdapter` interface:

```
public class AutofacAdapter :
  ServiceStack.Configuration.IContainerAdapter
{

  private readonly Autofac.IContainer _container;

  public AutofacAdapter(Autofac.IContainer container)
  {
    this._container = container;
  }

  public T Resolve<T>()
  {
    return this._container.Resolve<T>();
  }

  public T TryResolve<T>()
  {
    T result;
  if (this._container.TryResolve<T>(out result))
    {
    return result;
    }
  return default(T);
  }
}
```

The adapter is then used as follows:

```
public override void Configure(Funq.Container container)
{
  var containerBuilder = Autofac.ContainerBuilder();
  // TODO all the plumbing is done here
  var autofacAdapter = new AutofacAdapter(containerBuilder.Build());
  container.Adapter = autofacAdapter;
}
```

This makes the adapter responsible to abstract the resolving, whereas the injected container holds the registrations. The constructor parameters are resolved with the `Resolve<T>()` method, whereas property injection is done by a call to the `TryResolve<T>()` method.

You can further customize your adapter by implementing the `ServiceStack.Configuration.IRelease` interface to release objects, which implement the `System.IDisposable` interface, from the container when a request ends. This happens before the container gets disposed by the `AppHost.Release` method.

Incorporating the IoC container in your application

One of the key features of IoC is that it lets the container construct your object and apply the needed auto-wiring. For a ServiceStack service this is quite trivial, as the pipeline resolves the properties of your service for the request accordingly via Funq. The default lifetime of a service instance is `Funq.ReuseScope.None`, which creates a new service instance for every request.

You can get around the limited lifetime of your service by overriding the registration while configuring your application host, as shown:

```
public override void Configure(Funq.Container
container)
{
  container.RegisterAutoWired<TaskService>()
          .ReusedWithin(Funq.ReuseScope.Hierarchy);
}
```

However, the container can also be used outside the scope of your service. A bundled resolver is available for the **ASP.NET MVC** framework, to provide construction and injection of controller instances that can be configured as:

```
usingServiceStack.Mvc;

public override void Configure(Funq.Container container)
{
  var funqControllerFactory = new FunqControllerFactory(container);
  var controllerBuilder = System.Web.Mvc.ControllerBuilder.Current;
  controllerBuilder.SetFactory(funqControllerFactory);
}
```

This overrides the factory of the `ControllerBuilder` instance to Funq.

For **ASP.NET WebForms,** you need to do some more work that involves the creation of a custom handler factory as well as some adaptions in the `web.config` file, as shown in the following code:

```
using System.Web ;
using System.Web.UI;
using ServiceStack;

public class ServiceStackPageHandlerFactory : PageHandlerFactory
{
  public override IHttpHandler GetHandler(HttpContext httpContext,
                                          string requestType,
                                          string virtualPath,
                                          string path)
  {
  var httpHandler = base.GetHandler(httpContext,
                                    requestType,
                                    virtualPath,
                                    path);

    ServiceStackHost.Instance.Container.AutoWire(httpHandler);

    return httpHandler;
  }
}
```

The `ServiceStackPageHandlerFactory` object loops the creation of the concrete handler through to the framework's `PageHandlerFactory` and applies auto-wiring for all registered dependencies.

```
<configuration>
  <system.webServer>
    <handlers>
      <add name="ServiceStackPageHandlerFactory"
           path="*.aspx"
           verb="*"
           type="ServiceStackPageHandlerFactory, MyAssembly" />
    </handlers>
  </system.webServer>
</configuration>
```

This adaption of the `web.config` file defines the `ServiceStackPageHandlerFactory` class as the factory for all requests against `.aspx` files for any HTTP verb (GET, POST …).

This method comes with one caveat though; you cannot use constructor injection, as the concrete handlers are still constructed in the base class by internal methods of `System.Web.BuildManager`.

You can take this example further by deriving your MVC controller from `ServiceStack.Mvc.ServiceStackController` or your ASP.NET page from `ServiceStack.AspNet.SeriveStackPage`.

This gives you a shorthand access to all the ServiceStack components, such as Session, Cache, MQ, and many others. You can even add `ServiceStack.AuthenticateAttribute`, `ServiceStack.RequiredRoleAttribute`, and `ServiceStack.RequiredPremissionAttribute` attributes to your controller or page to do straightforward access checks.

The Ticket application

It is much more advisable to discuss problems and solutions with the help of a working example. Therefore, we will create a basic application to handle tickets (without any workflow), which we will expand throughout the course of this chapter.

The application will initially be implemented by the following RESTful web services:

1. `TicketService`: Create, read, update, and delete tickets.
2. `CommentService`: Administer comments of tickets (create, read, update, and delete).

Whenever you are dealing with multiple entities it is a good idea to use the rule of thumb and separate the services based on the handled entities.

The implementation of this example has been done by following the **Test Driven Development** (TDD) approach. It's done by designing the domain layer and then consecutively implementing the subjacent layers based on the red-green-refactor mantra. The implementation phase is covered by Unit Tests against each iteration. The actual code is available in the code folder of this book.

Domain design

One of the key points of ServiceStack is the Code-First approach. This gives us the opportunity to take care of the domain modeling before we design the database.

Following the **DRY (Don't Repeat Yourself)** principle we will reuse the POCOs in our whole architecture – from the database to the API.

There is a recent summary of this approach by Demis Bellot, which is available at http://stackoverflow. com/a/32940275/57508.

The ticket model

The following class represents the ticket model:

```
public partial class Ticket
{
  [ServiceStack.DataAnnotations.AutoIncrement]
  public int Id { get; set; }
  public ulong RowVersion { get; set; }
  public string Title { get; set; }
  public Status Status { get; set; }
}
public enum Status
{
  Active,
  Completed
}
```

The UML notation of the preceding code is as follows:

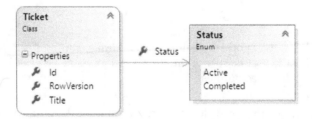

A `Ticket` class consists of a `Title` and an `Id` property, which is automatically created by the system through the `AutoIncrement` attribute. It holds a `RowVersion` property to ensure **optimistic concurrency**, which is a naive approach to solve the problem of conflicting modifications or lost updates. A ticket can be either **Active** or **Completed**, which is represented through its `Status` property.

The comment model

A `Comment` is a very simple class, consisting of a `Text`, an auto-generated `Id`, and a `RowVersion` property.

```
public partial class Comment
{
   [ServiceStack.DataAnnotations.AutoIncrement]
   public int Id { get; set; }
   public ulong RowVersion { get; set; }
   public string TicketId { get; set; }
   public string Text { get; set; }
}
```

The UML notation of the preceding code is as follows:

One main issue in distributed systems is the non-atomic nature: Two users save the same entity at the same time – both succeed as the writing to the database is done back-to-back, but one write operation gets overridden by the other, leaving one local entity out of date.

There are many solutions to such collisions, such as locking, conflict resolving by the user, merging, and many others.

The reason why we are using optimistic concurrency here is that it comes built-in with ServiceStack and it's a common solution incorporated in many frameworks (such as Bugzilla, Google App Engine, Elasticsearch, Apache CouchDB, Redis, and many more).

A good starting point to dive deeper into this topic is available at `http://www.agiledata.org/essays/concurrencyControl.html`.

RESTful design

The service exposes two endpoints (for `Tickets` and `Comments`) that are defined by a very clear URI structure and appropriate HTTP verbs.

The TicketService API

The following table shows an overview of the available operations of the service:

URI	HTTP verb	Description
`/tickets`	`GET`	Gets the list of tickets.
`/tickets/{id}`	`GET`	Gets the details of a ticket.
`/tickets`	`POST`	Creates a new ticket.
`/tickets/{id}`	`PUT`	Updates a ticket instance.
`/tickets/{id}`	`DELETE`	Deletes a ticket.

These URIs correspond to the following RequestDTOs:

```
using System.Collections.Generic;
using ServiceStack;

public class GetTickets :IReturn<List<Ticket>>
{
}

public class GetTicket :IReturn<Ticket>
{
```

```
    public int Id { get; set; }
  }

  public class StoreTicket : IReturn<Ticket>
  {
    public int Id { get; set; }
    public ulong RowVersion { get; set; }
    public string Title { get; set; }
    public Status Status { get; set; }
  }

  public class DeleteTicket : IReturnVoid
  {
    public int Id { get; set; }
  }
```

These RequestDTOs are registered with the following adaptions to the Configure method:

```
  public override void Configure(Funq.Container container)
  {
    this.Routes.Add<GetTickets>("/tickets",
                                ApplyTo.Get)
        .Add<StoreTicket>("/tickets",
                                ApplyTo.Post)
        .Add<StoreTicket>("/tickets/{Id}",
                                ApplyTo.Put)
        .Add<GetTicket>("/tickets/{Id}",
                          ApplyTo.Get)
        .Add<DeleteTicket>("/tickets/{Id}",
                                ApplyTo.Delete);
  }
```

The CommentService API

The following table shows an overview of the available methods of the service:

URI	HTTP verb	Description
/tickets/{id}/comments	GET	Gets the list of comments of a ticket.
/tickets/{id}/comments	POST	Creates a new comment.
/tickets/{id}/comments/{id}	PUT	Updates a comment.
/tickets/{id}/comments/{id}	DELETE	Deletes a comment.

These URIs correspond to the following RequestDTOs:

```
using System.Collections.Generic;
using ServiceStack;

public class GetComments : IReturn<List<Comment>>
{
  public int TicketId { get; set; }
}

public class StoreComment : IReturn<Comment>
{
  public int Id { get; set; }
  public ulong RowVersion { get; set; }
  public int TicketId { get; set; }
  public string Text { get; set; }
}

public class DeleteComment : IReturnVoid
{
  public int Id { get; set; }
  public int TicketId { get; set; }
}
```

These RequestDTOs are registered with the following adaptions to the `Configure` method:

```
public override void Configure(Funq.Container container)
{
  this.Routes.Add<GetComments>("/tickets/{TicketId}/comments",
                    ApplyTo.Get)
      .Add<StoreComment>("/tickets/{TicketId}/comments",
                    ApplyTo.Post)
      .Add<StoreComment>("/tickets/{TicketId}/comments/{Id}",
                    ApplyTo.Put)
      .Add<DeleteComment>("/tickets/{TicketId}/comments/{Id}",
                    ApplyTo.Delete);
}
```

After the creation of a RequestDTO you have to register the instance in the matching service. This is usually done by implementing for example `ServiceStack.IGet<T>`, which only registers an implicit route for your handling method. For a RESTful design you should register the REST paths, which is done by either annotating methods with `ServiceStack.RouteAttribute` or registering a route, as shown in the preceding examples. Depending on the scenario, either approach is acceptable as long as you follow your chosen path with consistency. If you plan to give away the assembly with all the RequestDTOs and POCOs, you can avoid the imposition of ServiceStack dependencies by registering the routes in your `Configure` method.

Data access

At this moment the repositories will simply follow the scheme of **create**, **read**, **update**, and **delete** (**CRUD**). To keep our focus on domain implementation, we will stick with an in-memory database for now, which is abstracted by the `TicketRepository` class and `CommentRepository` class.

Functional contract testing

For a brief functional test and to show off the optimistic concurrency feature of our application, we will create a simple suite of some tests.

```
using Funq;
using NUnit.Framework;
using ServiceStack;
using ServiceStack.Data;
using ServiceStack.OrmLite;
using System;
using System.Reflection;

public class TestAppHost : AppSelfHostBase
{
  public TestAppHost(
  params Assembly[] assembliesWithService)
      : base("Test App Host", assembliesWithService) { }

  public Action<Container> ConfigureContainer { get; set; }
```

```
  public override void Configure(Container container)
  {
    if (this.ConfigureContainer != null)
    {
      this.ConfigureContainer.Invoke(container);
    }
  }
}


[TestFixture]
public class AppHostFunctionalTests
{
  private const string URLBase = "http://localhost:1337/";
  privateServiceStackHost _appHost;

  [TestFixtureSetUp]
  public void TestFixtureSetUp()
  {
    this._appHost = new TestAppHost(typeof (TicketSerivce).Assembly)
    {
      ConfigureContainer = container =>
      {
        container.RegisterAutoWired<CommentRepository>()
                 .InitializedBy((c, repository) =>
                 repository.Initialize());
        container.RegisterAutoWired<TicketRepository>()
                 .InitializedBy((c, repository) =>
                 repository.Initialize());
        container.Register<IDbConnectionFactory>(arg => new
        OrmLiteConnectionFactory(":memory:",
        SqliteDialect.Provider));
      }
    }.Init()
     .Start(URLBase);
  }


  [TestFixtureTearDown]
  public void TestFixtureTearDown()
  {
    this._appHost.Dispose();
  }
}
```

This is the basic skeleton of our test, which uses a setup-method to initialize a host that is accessible over HTTP. To ensure access over HTTP we create a generic `TestAppHost`, which behaves very similarly to the `BasicAppHost` class in initialization matters. As mentioned earlier, we will use a very simple in-memory DBMS for our scenario, SQLite.

With the following simple test we have to create a new ticket and ensure that it got an automatically generated identifier from the database:

```
[Test]
public void ShouldCreateTicketAndListIt()
{
  using (var jsonServiceClient = new JsonServiceClient(URLBase))
  {
    var ticket = jsonServiceClient.Put(new StoreTicket
                                       {
                                         Title = "This is a
                                         ticket"
                                       });
    Assert.That(ticket.Id > 0);
    var tickets = jsonServiceClient.Get(new GetTickets());
    Assert.That(tickets.Count > 0);
  }
}
```

This next test creates a ticket instance and then tries to update it without providing a `RowVersion`. The resulting throw of a `WebServiceException` object is expected to occur:

```
[Test]
  public void ShouldCreateTicketButFailOnUpdate()
{
    using (var jsonServiceClient = new JsonServiceClient(URLBase))
    {
var ticketId = jsonServiceClient.Put(new StoreTicket
                                     {
                                       Title = "This is a ticket"
                                     });
    Assert.That(ticketId > 0);
    Assert.Throws<WebServiceException>(() =>
    jsonServiceClient.Post(new StoreTicket
                           {
                           Id = ticketId,
                           Title = "A new title"
                           }));
  }
}
```

In contrast the next test adds a version to the update request, which results in a successful update:

```
[Test]
public void ShouldCreateTicketAndUpdate()
{
  using (var jsonServiceClient = new JsonServiceClient(URLBase))
  {
  var ticket = jsonServiceClient.Put(new StoreTicket
  {
    Title = "This is a ticket"
  });
  Assert.That(ticket.Id > 0);
  ticket = jsonServiceClient.Post(new StoreTicket
    {
  Id = ticket.Id,
  RowVersion = ticket.RowVersion,
  Title = "A new title"
  });
  Assert.That(ticket.Id > 0);
  Assert.That(ticket.RowVersion > 1);
  }
}
```

Sessions

Whenever there's a need to store data that needs the scope of a (browser) session, the ordinary approach is to store data on the server-side, which can be accessed via a session-key that is stored on the client by some mechanism.

Three types of session lifetimes exist within a browser scenario. They are as follows:

- **Temporary sessions**: The cookie holding the session key has no explicit expiration timestamp set; hence, it lives only while a browser window is open.

- **Permanent sessions**: The session key is stored in a cookie, whose expiration timestamp is set in the far future (ServiceStack uses a lifetime of 20 years from creation as the default).

- **Sliding sessions**: The cookie that holds the session key is stored with an expiry in the near future. This expiration date is advanced by every following request; hence, it has the term **sliding** in its name.

To enable session support in your application, you need to register the session feature:

```
public override void Configure(Funq.Container container)
{
    this.Plugins.Add(new ServiceStack.SessionFeature());
}
```

This adds a delegate, which ensures the existence of cookies for the session key, to the `GlobalRequestFilters` property of your host. Additionally the keys are added to the `Items` property of the request to ease access.

 You can adapt the expiration time span by setting a value to the `PermanentSessionExpiry` or `SessionExpiry` property of the `SessionFeature` object.

ServiceStack supports the two former lifetimes out of the box, where temporary sessions are default. The session key is taken either from a temporary cookie `ss-id` or a permanent cookie `ss-pid`. A cookie with the name `ss-opt` (which has either `perm` or `temp` as its value) is used to toggle the actual used cookie. The permanent cookie `ss-id` is created anyway to provide the possibility to track requests regardless of the actual used lifetime.

As requests to web services are not always done within a browser, you can use custom HTTP headers to provide the session information along with your request. This is done by prepending `X-` to the name of the cookie as the header field name.

The logic behind the creation of a session key does not incorporate any information on the currently used server instance. This is in contrast to the native ASP.NET logic that hashes the value with the machine name. This makes setting up a shared session in a server farm with ServiceStack a more straightforward process.

 Internally, a `System.Security.Cryptography.RNGCryptoServiceProvider` instance is used to generate a random session key instead of utilizing a `System.Random` instance, as the provider gives an unpredictable and therefore safer seed instead of using `System.Environment.TickCount`. Another reason is the flawed implementation of `System.Random` – more information available at `https://connect.microsoft.com/VisualStudio/feedback/details/634761/system-random-serious-bug` and `http://stackoverflow.com/a/6842191/57508`.

Session sharing between your service and a web application

ServiceStack provides its own implementation of a session due to the tight and untestable implementation of sessions in the ASP.NET framework, which also faces some serious performance issues.

 More information on the performance issues is available at `http://stackoverflow.com/q/3629709/57508`.

When you are introducing ServiceStack to an already existing ASP.NET web application and you want to access sessions in both the frameworks, you have the following two options to choose from.

Using the ServiceStack session

This can be easily achieved simply by deriving your page from `ServiceStack.AspNet.SeriveStackPage` or your controller from `ServiceStack.Mvc.ServiceStackController`, giving you simple access to the session with the `SessionBag` property:

```
var foo = this.SessionBag.Get<Foo>(fooKey);
this.SessionBag.Set(fooKey, foo);
this.SessionBag.Remove(fooKey);
this.SessionBag.RemoveAll();
```

 This approach doesn't give you the possibility to do a cookie-less authentication with query string parameters. You would have to implement your own request filter to inject the session key from the requested URL to the `Items` collection of your request and provide a method to adapt your generated hyperlinks.

I strongly recommend this approach, as it gets you around the limitations of the ASP.NET session.

Using the ASP.NET session

As the engine of ASP.NET only adds the session to handlers, which implement the `System.Web.SessionState.IRequiresSessionState` interface, you need to create a wrapper class for any of the ServiceStack handlers.

This wrapper is then returned by the `GetHandler` method of the `LegacySessionHttpHandlerFactory` class:

```
using ServiceStack;
using System.Web;
using System.Web.SessionState;

public class LegacySessionHttpHandlerFactory : IHttpHandlerFactory
{
  private static readonly HttpHandlerFactory HttpHandlerFactory =
  new HttpHandlerFactory();

  public IHttpHandler GetHandler(HttpContext context,
                                 string requestType,
                                 string url,
                                 string pathTranslated)
  {
  var handler = HttpHandlerFactory.GetHandler(context,
                                              requestType,
                                              url,
                                              pathTranslated);
  if (handler != null)
    {
    handler = new LegacySessionHttpHandler(handler);
    }
  return null;
  }
}

public class LegacySessionHttpHandler : IHttpHandler,
                                        IRequiresSessionState
{
  private readonly IHttpHandler _handler;

  public LegacySessionHttpHandler(IHttpHandler handler)
  {
    this._handler = handler;
  }

  public IHttpHandler Handler
  {
    get
    {
```

```
      return this._handler;
    }
  }

  public bool IsReusable
  {
    get
    {
     return this.Handler.IsReusable;
    }
  }

  public void ProcessRequest(HttpContext context)
  {
    this.Handler.ProcessRequest(context);
  }
}
```

Additionally, you have to exchange the factory in the `handlers` element in the `web.config` file:

```
<system.webServer>
  <handlers>
    <add path="*"
         verb="*"
         name="LegacySessionHttpHandlerFactory"
         type="LegacySessionHttpHandlerFactory, MyAssembly"
         preCondition="integrated"
         resourceType="Unspecified"
         allowPathInfo="true" />
  </handlers>
</system.webServer>
```

Now, to access the legacy session in the ServiceStack scope, you have to create a custom session:

```
using System.Web;
using System.Web.SessionState;
using ServiceStack.Caching;

public class LegacySession : ISession
{
  public HttpSessionState Session
  {
```

```
    get
    {
      return HttpContext.Current.Session;
    }
  }

  public void Set<T>(string key, T value)
  {
    this[key] = value;
  }

  public T Get<T>(string key)
  {
    return (T) this[key];
  }

  public bool Remove(string key)
  {
    this.Session.Remove(key);
    return true; // naive approach
  }

  public void RemoveAll()
  {
    this.Session.RemoveAll();
  }

  public object this[string key]
  {
    get
    {
      return this.Session[key];
    }
    set
    {
      this.Session[key] = value;
    }
  }
}
```

Finally, you have to register the LegacySession class in the IoC container, as shown:

```
public override void Configure(Funq.Container container)
{
  container.RegisterAutoWiredAs<LegacySession,
  ServiceStack.Caching.ISession>()
             .ReusedWithin(Funq.ReuseScope.Request);
}
```

The other option to inject LegacySession, is to roll your own ServiceStack. Caching.ISessionFactory:

```
using ServiceStack;
using ServiceStack.Caching;
using ServiceStack.Web;

public class LegacySessionFactory : ISessionFactory
{
  public ISession GetOrCreateSession(IRequest httpReq,
                                     IResponse htttRes)
  {
    return new LegacySession();
  }

  public ISession GetOrCreateSession()
  {
    var httpReq = HostContext.GetCurrentRequest();
    var httpRes = httpReq.Response;
    return this.GetOrCreateSession(httpReq,
                                   httpRes);
  }
}
```

Cache

Additional to the session data, any serializable object can be saved in a cache, which is a common technique to speed up applications. Therefore, ServiceStack offers the following cache clients:

- ServiceStack.Redis.RedisClientManagerCacheClient:

```
container.Register<IRedisClientManager>(arg =>
  newPooledRedisClientManager());
container.Register(arg =>
  arg.Resolve<IRedisClientManager>().GetCacheClient());
```

- ServiceStack.Caching.Memcached.MemcachedClientCache:

  ```
  container.Register<ICacheClient>(arg => new
      MemcachedClientCache());
  ```

- ServiceStack.Caching.Azure.AzureCacheClient:

  ```
  container.Register<ICacheClient>(arg => new
      AzureCacheClient());
  ```

- ServiceStack.Caching.AwsDynamoDb.DynamoDbCacheClient:

  ```
  container.Register<ICacheClient>(arg => new
      DynamoDbCacheClient(...));
  ```

- ServiceStack.Caching.OrmLiteCacheClient:

  ```
  container.Register<ICacheClient>(arg => new
      OrmLiteCacheClient())
              .InitializeBy((arg, cacheClient) =>
              cacheClient.InitSchema());
  ```

- ServiceStack.Caching.MemoryCacheClient:

  ```
  container.Register<ICacheClient>(arg => new
      MemoryCacheClient());
  ```

There are additional interfaces available to mark a cache client and make it capable of special behavior:

- ICacheClientExtendend: It declares GetTimeToLive(string), which is used to query the remaining time span until the cache entry expires. Additionally GetKeysByPattern (string) is declared, which returns a collection of matching keys.

- IRemoveByPattern: Declares the RemoveAll method, that passes sess:{sessionId}:* for the removal of all keys and their corresponding values.

Caching session data

The bundled ServiceStack.SessionFactory expects an ICacheClient instance for construction, which is used to persist data. To store items on the provided cache client, an identifier is computed and every item is stored in the session with a key that is prefixed by sess:{sessionId}:. The resulting key is taken for persisting the value, as shown here:

```
this.SessionBag.Set("foo", new Foo());
// the key used will be sess:{sessionId}:foo
var foo = this.SessionBag.Get<Foo>("foo");
```

As the session key is added to the name of the cache entry, a collision between different sessions is avoided.

You can also store globally available data directly in the cache by utilizing the
Cache property of a service. Note that no prefixing takes place and the usage of
ServiceStack.Common.UrnId is highly recommended in order to avoid collision:

```
this.Cache.Add(UrnId.Create<Foo>(string.Empty),
                new Foo());
this.Cache.Add(UrnId.Create<Foo>(string.Empty),
                new Foo(), TimeSpan.FromMinutes(20d));
var item = this.Cache.Get<Foo>("foo");
```

Caching responses

To store results of service methods in the cache, you can use the
ToOptimizedResultUsingCache method on the Request property of your service.

```
public object Get(GetTickets request)
{
  var tickets = this.Request.ToOptimizedResultUsingCache(this.Cache,
    UrnId.Create<GetTickets>(string.Empty),
    () =>this.Repository.Read());
  return tickets;
}
```

You can also add an expiration timestamp to the cache entry, which will remove an
expired cache entry on the next request after expiry.

```
public object Get(GetTickets request)
{
var tickets = this.Request.ToOptimizedResultUsingCache(this.Cache,
    UrnId.Create<GetTickets>(string.Empty),
TimeSpan.FromMinutes(20d),
    () =>this.Repository.Read());
return tickets;
}
```

In contrast to this approach, there's also the possibility to manually invalidate a cache
entry. For example, if you delete some data, the corresponding retrieval methods
should return an updated output, as shown here:

```
public void Delete(DeleteTicket request)
{
  this.Request.RemoveFromCache(this.Cache,
```

```
        UrnId.Create<GetTickets>(request.Id),
        UrnId.Create<GetTickets>(string.Empty));
    this.Repository.Delete(request);
}
```

The cached responses are deleted immediately, so that the provided delegate in the `ToOptimizedResultUsingCache` method call is executed again on the next request.

Authentication and authorization

These two terms are normally applied to sensible endpoints, where "authentication" is all about getting the information about which user executes a requests, and "authorization" checks if the authenticated user is allowed to request a resource.

Authentication providers

Based on your authentication method you can choose from the following available providers (all implementing the `ServiceStack.Auth.IAuthProvider` interface):

- **Basic providers**: These providers depend on a registered `ServiceStack.Auth.IAuthRepository` implementation to ensure authentication:

    ○ `ServiceStack.Auth.CredentialsProvider`: You can obtain an authenticated session, by posting a username and a password (either via query string parameters or JSON payload) to `/auth/credentials`.

    ○ `ServiceStack.Auth.BasicAuthProvider`: Adding an HTTP header `Authorization` (according to RFC 1945 for HTTP 1.0 and 2617 for HTTP 1.1) to the request triggers the validation of the provided credentials to obtain an authenticated session.

    ○ `ServiceStack.Auth.DigestAuthProvider`: This provider is a more secure version of `BasicAuthProvider`, as a hashing method is used instead of sending the password in plain text.

    ○ `ServiceStack.Auth.AspNetWindowsAuthProvider`: This provider checks the provided **NT Lan Manager** (**NTLM**) authentication information of the request to be authenticated.

- **OAuth providers**: OAuth is an open protocol that leverages an external service for authentication and authorization, where you need to procure a key to sign the requests to be able to access data from the service. You can even implement your own provider by deriving from the `ServiceStack.Auth.OAuthProvider` class:

    ○ `ServiceStack.Auth.FacebookAuthProvider`

    ○ `ServiceStack.Auth.GithubAuthProvier`

    ○ `ServiceStack.Auth.OndoklassnikiAuthProvider`

    ○ `ServiceStack.Auth.TwitterAuthProvider`

    ○ `ServiceStack.Auth.YammerAuthProvider`

    ○ `ServiceStack.Auth.YandexAuthProvider`

    ○ `ServiceStack.Auth.VkAuthProvider`

- **OAuth2 providers** (available via `ServiceStack.Authentication.OAuth2` NuGet package). OAuth2 is the further development of OAuth, to reduce complexity and provide modularity. You can implement your own provider by deriving from `ServiceStack.Authentication.OAuth2.OAuth2Provider`:

    ○ `ServiceStack.Authentication.OAuth2.FourSquareOAuth2Provider`

    ○ `ServiceStack.Authentication.OAuth2.GoogleOAuth2Provider`

    ○ `ServiceStack.Authentication.OAuth2.InstagramOAuth2Provider`

    ○ `ServiceStack.Authentication.OAuth2.LinkedInOAuth2Provider`

    ○ `ServiceStack.Authentication.OAuth2.MicrosoftLiveOAuth2Provider`

- **OpenId providers** (available via `ServiceStack.Authentication.OpenId` NuGet package). OpenId is a decentralized alternative to OAuth providers when you only need authentication. You can implement your own provider by deriving from `ServiceStack.Authentication.OpenId.OpenIdOAuthProvider`:

    ○ `ServiceStack.Authentication.OpenId.GoogleOpenIdOAuthProvider`

    ○ `ServiceStack.Authentication.OpenId.MyOpenIdOAuthProvider`

    ○ `ServiceStack.Authentication.OpenId.YahooOpenIdOAuthProvider`

When you are going for a basic provider it is absolutely necessary to add SSL to your public endpoints. This will secure the HTTP headers and payloads, leaving the URL as a vector for an attack. Therefore, ensure that the credentials are not provided by query string parameters, which might be included in the initial HTTP request of an HTTPS handshake!

Authentication repository

The next step is to decide which `ServiceStack.Auth.IAuthRepository` implementation to use. Besides the possibility of implementing your own repository, you have plenty of options to choose from:

- `ServiceStack.Auth.InMemoryAuthRepository`: This is the default repository used to store data. Due to its nature, data is not persisted and is lost after an AppDomain restarts.

- `ServiceStack.Auth.RedisAuthRepository`: A repository for Redis.

- `ServiceStack.Auth.OrmLiteAuthRepository`: An OrmLite repository to access any supported DBMS by OrmLite.

- `ServiceStack.Auth.RavenDb.RavenDbUserAuthRepository` (`ServiceStack.Authentication.RavenDb` package): A repository to access authentication with RavenDb.

- `ServiceStack.Authentication.NHibernate.` `NHibernateUserAuthRepository` (`ServiceStack.Authenication.` `NHibernate` package): A NHibernate repository to access authentication with any supported DBMS by NHibernate.

- `ServiceStack.Authentication.MongoDb.MongoDbAuthRepository` (`ServiceStack.Authentication.MongoDb` package):A repository to access authentication with MongoDb.

The implementation of the `IAuthRepository` interface is the best starting point to add a connection to an already existing database with user entities. You can simply implement your own repository and loop the queries through to your storage:

- `void LoadUserAuth (IAuthSession session, IAuthTokens tokens)`: This method is responsible to populate the provided `session` parameter with detailed data of the user entity.

- `void SaveUserAuth(IAuthSessionauthSession)`: This method adapts the `ModifiedDate` property of the corresponding `IUserAuth` or creates a new one.

- `List<IUserAuthDetails>GetUserAuthDetails(string userAuthId)`: This returns the detailed data of a user entity.

- `IUserAuthDetails CreateOrMergeAuthSession(IAuthSession authSession, IAuthTokens tokens)`: Creates a user entity or merges the changes from a user session to it.

- `IUserAuth GetUserAuth(IAuthSession authSession, IAuthTokens tokens)`: Returns a user entity for the user session.

- `IUserAuth GetUserAuthByName(string userNameOrEmail)`: Returns a matching user entity.

- `void SaveUserAuth(IUserAuth userAuth)`: Saves a user entity.

- `bool TryAuthenticate(string userName, string password, out IUserAuth userAuth)`: Tries to get a user entity that matches the user name and password.

- `bool TryAuthenticate(Dictionary<string, string> digestHeaders, string privateKey, int nonceTimeout, string sequence, out IUserAuth userAuth)`: This method is used for digest authentication and tries to return a matching user entity.

Limiting access

To limit the access to your service you have the following options:

- Annotate a service with `ServiceStack.AuthenticateAttribute`

- Annotate any method of a service with `ServiceStack.AuthenticateAttribute`

- Annotate a RequestDTO with `ServiceStack.AuthenticateAttribute`

- Inject a `ServiceStack.AuthenticateAttribute` object in a request filter:

```
public override void Configure(Funq.Container container)
{
  this.GlobalRequestFilters.Add((httpReq,
                                 httpRes,
                                 dto) =>
  {
    var authenticateAttribute = new AuthenticateAttribute();
    authenticateAttribute.Execute(httpReq,
                                  httpRes,
                                  dto);
  });
}
```

Additionally to authentication you can further limit the access by annotating resources with `ServiceStack.RequiredRoleAttribute`, `ServiceStack.RequiresAnyRoleAttribute`, `ServiceStack.RequiredPermissionAttribute`, and `ServiceStack.RequiresAnyPermissionAttribute`.

 You can implement your own attributes by deriving from `AuthenticateAttribute` to limit access. This gives you the possibility to customize authentication by overriding the `Execute(IRequest, IResponse, object)` method.

 Another benefit of incorporating `ServiceStackPage` or `ServiceStackController` in your design, is that you can decorate your pages and controllers with the attributes shown to limit access, as they are taken into account on execution.

Processing chain

In general processing chain has the following steps:

1. The need for authentication is determined before the request handler is executed.

2. If an `AuthenticateAttribute` is found to be responsible for the request, its `Execute` method is called.

3. The `IAuthSession` that corresponds to the session key is read from the cache or created.

4. The matching provider 's `IsAuthorized` method is called.

5. If the current session is not authorized, an HTTP redirect is issued (if configured) and the `OnFailedAuthentication` event is triggered.

6. If the session is authorized and a `RequiredRoleAttribute` does apply, its `Execute` method is called to check the role of the session against the stated one. If this probing fails, an `HTTP 403` `(Forbidden: Invalid Role)` response is issued.

7. Additionally, if a `RequiredPermissionAttribute` applies, its `Execute` method is called to check the permission. If this probing fails, an `HTTP 403` `(Forbidden: Invalid Permission)` response is issued.

The processing of provided credentials is done in the provider, which reads the data and validates it against an `IAuthProvider` instance (with the help of `ServiceStack.Auth.AuthenticateService` for the basic providers).

When the user is authenticated, the user data is stored as a special `ServiceStack.Auth.IAuthSession` in the cache for a limited period of time (where the default is 20 minutes).

Adding authentication and authorization to the Ticket application

Firstly, we need to register and configure the `AuthFeature`:

```
using Funq;
using ServiceStack;
using ServiceStack.Auth;
using ServiceStack.Data;

public override void Configure(Funq.Container container)
{
   this.Plugins.Add(new AuthFeature(() => new AuthUserSession(),
                             new IAuthProvider[]
                             {
                                new BasicAuthProvider()
                             }));
   container.Register<IAuthRepository>(arg => new
   OrmLiteAuthRepository(arg.Resolve<IDbConnectionFactory>()))
         .InitializedBy((arg, authRepository) =>
         {
            var userAuthRepository = (IUserAuthRepository)
            authRepository;
            userAuthRepository.InitSchema();
   if (userAuthRepository.GetUserAuthByUserName("johndoe") == null)
            {
               var userAuth = new UserAuth
                           {
                              UserName = "johndoe",
                              FirstName = "John",
                              LastName = "Doe"
                           };
               userAuthRepository.CreateUserAuth(userAuth,
                                          "password");
            }
         });
}
```

This registers the `AuthUserSession` class as the concrete authorization session and utilizes `BasicAuthProvider` to expect the credentials. Additionally, the `OrmLiteAuthRepository` is used as the data store and seeded with a demo user *johndoe*.

Now, we can utilize the `Authenticate` attribute to secure our service

```
using ServiceStack;

[Authenticate]
public class TicketService : Service
```

This gives us the opportunity to incorporate a processing user to our tickets that can then be injected into our service method `Put (StoreTicket)`:

```
using ServiceStack;

public partial class Ticket
{
  public string ProcessorUserAuthId { get; set; }
}

public object Put(StoreTicket request)
{
  var userAuthId = this.GetSession().UserAuthId;
  var ticket = request.ConvertTo<Ticket>();
  ticket.ProcessorUserAuthId = userAuthId;
  ticket = this.Repository.Store(ticket);
  this.Request.RemoveFromCache(this.Cache,
                              UrnId.Create<GetTicket>(ticket.Id),
                              UrnId.Create<GetTickets>
                              (userAuthId));
  return ticket;
}
```

Moreover, the processor is introduced as another scope in the caching strategy. To fix our tests for retrieval of the ticket list, we need to inject the basic authentication, as shown:

```
[Test]
public void ShouldGetTickets()
{
  using (var jsonServiceClient = new ServiceStack.
  JsonServiceClient(URLBase))
  {
```

```
jsonServiceClient.UserName = "johndoe";
jsonServiceClient.Password = "password";
var tickets = jsonServiceClient.Get(new GetTickets());
Assert.That(tickets != null);
    }
}
```

Now the test passes again. Additionally, we also have to add the credentials to other tests to make them pass again.

Extending authentication and authorization

The following examples are starting points for how to further extend authentication with ServiceStack:

Sliding authentication

There are many ways to implement a sliding session for authentication with ServiceStack, each targeting the expiration of the cache entry instead of the cookie. One way, suggested by Demis Bellot – Project lead of ServiceStack – is to introduce a response filter:

```
public override void Configure(Funq.Container container)
{
  this.GlobalResponseFilters.Add((httpReq,
                                  httpRes,
                                  dto) =>
  {
    var session = httpReq.GetSession();
              httpReq.SaveSession(session,
              TimeSpan.FromMinutes(20d));
  }
}
```

Extending the authentication session

There are several reasons to implement a customized ServiceStack.Auth. IAuthSession. The only thing you have to keep in mind is that when you are deriving from the ServiceStack.AuthUserSession class you have to annotate your customized session class with System.Runtime.Serialization. DataContractAttribute and System.Runtime.Serialization. DataMemberAttribute, in order to keep the class serializable:

```
using ServiceStack;
using System.Runtime.Serialization;
```

```
[DataContract]
public class CustomAuthUserSession : AuthUserSession
{
  [DataMember]
  public sting CustomData { get; set; }
}
```

Additionally, you have to adapt the registration of the `AuthFeature`:

```
public override void Configure(Funq.Container container)
{
  this.Plugins.Add(new AuthFeature(() => new CustomAuthUserSession(),
                          new IAuthProvider []
             {
               new BasicAuthProvider()
             });
}
```

This adapts the factory delegate for sessions in the plugin. You can now access the custom session in your service with `this.SessionAs<CustomAuthUserSession>()`.

Since sessions are stored in the cache, you also have to adapt the serialization and deserialization process to reflect the custom type—except if `InMemoryAuthRepository` is used as your repository. Therefore, you need to ensure that the type information does not get omitted by ensuring it with `JsConfig<CustomAuthUserSession>.IncludeTypeInfo = true`. Additionally, if you want to adapt the values of properties, you have to call `this.SaveSession(IAuthSession)` to persist the changes to the repository.

Customizing the user entity

Whenever you extend your user session, adaptions to the user entity within the repository are inevitable. The following example covers the adaptions that need to be made on the `OrmLiteAuthRepository`:

```
using ServiceStack.Auth;

public class CustomUserAuth : UserAuth
{
  public virtual string CustomData { get; set; }
}
public class CustomUserAuthDetails : UserAuthDetails
{
```

```
    public virtual string CustomData { get; set; }
}

public override void Configure(Funq.Container container)
{
    container.Register<IAuthRepository>(arg => new
    OrmLiteAuthRepository<CustomUserAuth,
    CustomUserAuthDetails>(arg.Resolve<IDbConnectionFactory>()));
}
```

Authentication events

ServiceStack offers hooks to intercept any interaction with the user session.
There are two ways to implement this:

1. Implementing your own `ServiceStack.Auth.IAuthSession`.

2. Injecting an implementation of `ServiceStack.Auth.IAuthEvents` to
    the IoC container.

Both options offer the same descriptive hook.

```
void OnRegistered(IRequest,IAuthSession,IServiceBase)
void OnAuthenticated(IServiceBace,IAuthSession,IAuthTokens,
    Dictionary<string, string>)
void OnLogout(IServiceBase)
void OnCreated(IRequest)
```

Creating a custom authentication provider

The fact that ServiceStack is easily extendable plays perfectly into our hands when
we try to implement our own provider for authentication.

At first, we will create a custom provider:

```
using System.Collections.Generic;
using ServiceStack;
using ServiceStack.Auth;
using ServiceStack.Web;

public class CustomAuthProvider : CredentialsAuthProvider,
                                  IAuthWithRequest
{
    public new static string Name = "custom";
    public new static string Realm = "/auth/" + Name;

    public CustomAuthProvider()
```

```
{
  this.Provider = Name;
  this.AuthRealm = Realm;
}

public void PreAuthenticate(IRequest req,
                            IResponse res)
{
  SessionFeature.AddSessionIdToRequestFilter(req,
                                             res,
                                             null);
  var customAuth = this.GetCustomAuth(req);
  if (!customAuth.HasValue)
  {
    return;
  }

  var authService = req.TryResolve<AuthenticateService>();
  authService.Request = req;
  authService.Post(new Authenticate
                   {
                     provider = this.Provider,
                     UserName = customAuth.Value.Key,
                     Password = customAuth.Value.Value
                   });
}

public override object Authenticate(IServiceBase authService,
                                    IAuthSession session,
                                    Authenticate request)
{
  var httpReq = authService.Request;
  var customAuth = this.GetCustomAuth(httpReq);
  if (!customAuth.HasValue)
  {
    throw HttpError.Unauthorized(ErrorMessages.NotAuthenticated);
  }
  return this.Authenticate(authService,
                           session,
```

```
                                    customAuth.Value.Key,
                                    customAuth.Value.Value,
                                    request.Continue);
    }

    private KeyValuePair<string, string>? GetCustomAuth(IRequest
                                                        httpReq)
    {
      var userName = httpReq.GetHeader("X-UserName");
      var password = httpReq.GetHeader("X-Password");

      if (string.IsNullOrWhiteSpace(userName) ||
          string.IsNullOrWhiteSpace(password))
      {
        return null;
      }

      return new KeyValuePair<string, string>(userName, password);
    }
  }
```

This `CustomAuthProvider` class dervices from the `ServiceStack.Auth.` `CredentialsAuthProvider` class, which already covers a lot of implementation that we are going to need. Moreover, the custom provider implements the `ServiceStack.Auth.IAuthWithRequest` interface, which defines the `PreAuthenticate` method. This method is used to read attached authentication information from the request instead of requiring an explicit authentication request to /auth/custom. The `Authenticate` method is the handler for a request to /auth/custom and is also used from the `PreAuthenticate` method. To access the session id in our `PreAuthenticate` method, which is executed before the request filter of the `SessionFeature` that adds the session information to the request, we have to ensure the session by calling `SessionFeature.` `AddSessionIdToRequestFilter`.

Finally, we have to register the custom provider with the `AuthFeature`:

```
public override void Configure(Funq.Container container)
{
  this.Plugins.Add(new AuthFeature(() => new AuthUserSession(),
                                   new IAuthProvider[]
                                   {
                                      new CustomAuthProvider()
                                   }));
}
```

Provide credentials in RequestDTOs

This is not an approach I'd like to encourage, but sometimes you have to support the legacy roots.

First, we have to create an interface `IHasCredentials` that is implemented on the RequestDTOs to provide a username and password:

```
public interface IHasCredentials
{
   string UserName { get; set; }
   string Password { get; set; }
}
```

Finally, we just need to adapt the `GetCustomAuth` method of the previously introduced `CustomAuthProvider`:

```
private KeyValuePair<string, string>? GetCustomAuth(IRequest httpReq)
{
   var hasCredentials = httpReq.Dto as IHasCredentials;
   if (hasCredentials == null)
   {
     return null;
   }

   var userName = hasCredentials.UserName;
   var password = hasCredentials.Password;

   if (string.IsNullOrWhiteSpace(userName) ||
       string.IsNullOrWhiteSpace(password))
   {
     return null;
   }

   return new KeyValuePair<string, string>(userName, password);
}
```

 With these adaptions a request to `/auth/custom` will not work anymore, unless you provide a DTO that implements the `IHasCredentials` interface.

Authorization information in the HTTP header

Sometimes you just need to limit the access to a resource by a certain HTTP header that is not necessarily connected to authentication. The easiest approach is to create a custom attribute and decorate the resource in question to handle this scenario, as shown:

```
using System;
using ServiceStack;
using ServiceStack.Web;

[AttributeUsage(AttributeTargets.Class | AttributeTargets.Method)]
public class CustomAuthorizeAttribute : RequestFilterAttribute
{
  public override void Execute(IRequest req,
                               IResponse res,
                               object requestDto)
  {
    var token = req.GetHeader("X-Token");
    if (string.IsNullOrWhiteSpace(token))
    {
      throw HttpError.Unauthorized("Unauthorized");
    }
  }
}
```

You can now annotate classes and methods with this attribute, as implied by the `AttributeUsageAttribute` annotation.

Summary

In this chapter, the bundled IoC container Funq was introduced and the possibilities to inject your own container were shown. We set up a working demo to have a platform for adaptions and also had a look at the session and cache implementation. We now understand the connection between the two and how the data is persisted and retrieved. Finally, we explored the possibilities to secure our service with authentication and authorization.

In the next chapter, we will introduce asynchronous communication between components and introduce possibilities for two-way communication between processes.

3

Asynchronous Communication between Components

In this chapter we will cover the following topics:

- In Memory MQ
- RCON
- RedisMQ
- RabbitMQ
- Server-sent events
- Look left and right

The recent release of .NET has added several new ways to further embrace asynchronous and parallel processing by introducing the **Task Parallel Library** (**TPL**), `async`, and `await`.

The need for asynchronous processing is present since the early days of programming. Its main concept is to offload the processing to another thread or process to release the calling thread from waiting and it has become a standard model since the rise of GUIs.

In such interfaces only one thread is responsible for drawing the GUI, which must not be blocked in order to remain available and not putting the application in a non-responding state.

This paradigm is a core point in distributed systems, at some point, long running operations are offloaded to a separate component, either to overcome blocking or to avoid resource bottlenecks using dedicated machines, which also makes the processing more robust against unexpected application pool recycling and other such issues.

 A synonym for "fire-and-forget" is "one-way", which is also reflected by the design of static routes of ServiceStack endpoints, where the default is /{format}/oneway/{service}.

Asynchronism adds a whole new level of complexity to our processing chain, as some callers might depend on a return value. This problem can be overcome by adding callback or another event to your design, which callers can subscribe to.

Messaging or in general a producer-consumer chain is a fundamental design pattern, which can be applied within the same process or inter-process, on the same or a cross-machine to decouple components.

Consider the following architecture:

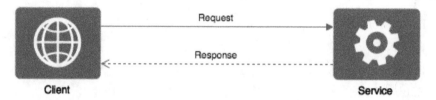

The client issues a request to the service, which processes the message and returns a response. The server is known and is directly bound to the client, which makes an on-the-fly addition of servers practically impossible. You'd need to reconfigure the clients to reflect the collection of servers at every change and implement a distribution logic for requests.

Therefore, a new component is introduced, which acts as a broker (without any processing of the message, except delivery) between the client and service to decouple the service from the client.

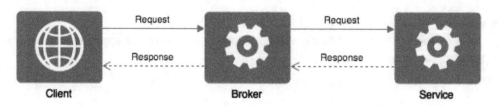

This gives us the opportunity to introduce more services for heavy load scenarios by simply registering a new instance to the broker, as shown in the following figure:

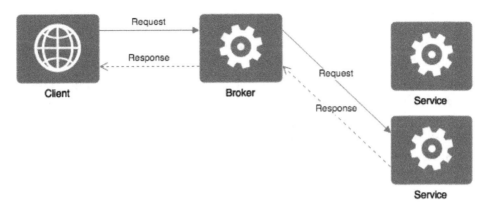

 I left out the clustering (scaling) of brokers and also the routing of messages on purpose at this stage of introduction.

In many cross process scenarios a database is introduced as a broker, which is constantly polled by services (and clients, if there's a response involved) to check whether there's a message to be processed or not. Adding a database as a broker and implementing your own logic can be absolutely fine for basic systems, but for more advanced scenarios it lacks some essential features, which Messages Queues come shipped with:

- **Scalability**: Decoupling is the biggest step towards a robust design, as it introduces the possibility to add more processing nodes to your data flow.

- **Resilience:** Messages are guaranteed to be delivered and processed as automatic retrying is available for non-acknowledged (processed) messages. If the retry count is exceeded, failed messages can be stored in a **Dead Letter Queue (DLQ)** to be inspected later and are requeued after fixing the issue that caused the failure. In case of a partial failure of your infrastructure, clients can still produce messages that get delivered and processed as soon as there is a single consumer back online.

- **Pushing instead of polling**: This is where asynchronism comes into play, as clients do not constantly poll for messages but instead get pushed by the broker when there's a new message in their subscribed queue.

- **Guaranteed order**: Most Message Queues offer a guaranteed order of the processing under defined conditions (mostly **FIFO**).

- **Load balancing**: With multiple handlers registered for messages, there is an inherent load balancing. In addition to this round-robin routing, there are other routing logics, such as smallest-mailbox, tail-chopping, or random routing.

- **Message persistence**: Message Queues can be configured to persist their data to disk and even survive restarts of the host on which they are running. To overcome the downtime of the Message Queue you can even set up a cluster to offload the demand to other brokers while restarting a single node.

- **Built-in priority**: Message Queues usually have separate queues for different messages and even provide a separate in queue for prioritized messages.

 There are many more features, such as Time to live, security and batching modes, which we will not cover as they are outside the scope of ServiceStack.

In the following example we will refer to two basic DTOs:

```
public class Hello : ServiceStack.IReturn<HelloResponse>
{
   public string Name { get; set; }
}
public class HelloResponse
{
   public string Result { get; set; }
}
```

The Hello class is used to send a Name to a consumer that generates a message, which will be then enqueued in the Message Queue as well.

In Memory MQ

The most basic implementation of messaging that is shipped with ServiceStack is a solution, which runs in the same process and memory, as shown in the following figure:

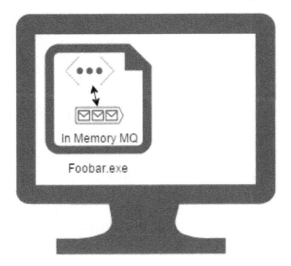

This queue offers you a simple in-process messaging with all the downsides that come with the linking of the process. For example, the messages will not survive an application restart as there's no storage implemented for the queue.

The factory, client, and server are located in the main ServiceStack NuGet package (ServiceStack.Messaging), as shown here:

```
using ServiceStack;
var inMemoryTransientMessageFactory = new
   ServiceStack.Messaging.InMemoryTransientMessageFactory();
var messageService =
   inMemoryTransientMessageFactory.CreateMessageService();

messageService.RegisterHandler<Hello>(message =>
{
   var hello = message.GetBody();
   var name = hello.Name;
   var helloResponse = new HelloResponse
                       {
                           Result = "Hello {0}".Fmt(name)
                       };
   return helloResponse;
});
messageService.Start();
```

This code creates a new factory that is used to create a broker within a process (this is different for all other messaging solutions as they leverage an external component for publishing and subscriptions).

Usually, you will bind the `messageService` object to a single context to guarantee a continuous processing throughout the runtime of your application. The easiest way, for example with ASP.NET, is to build the service within the start up in your `Global.asax` file and store it in a static field.

On this `messageService` object `RegisterHandler` is called, which registers a delegate as the handler of an incoming message. In fact this process is the same for all bundled Message Queue solutions, as they all are implemented by deriving from `ServiceStack.Messaging.IMessageService`. Within your delegate you have access to the message itself, as well as the captured DTO with a call to `GetBody`. The `Name` property is read and a welcome message is generated and returned to the broker. The concluding `Start` call starts the broker.

If you do not want to return an object to the broker, you can simply call `return null;` which makes the handler truly one way.

Adding another handler for printing the `HelloResponse` object to the console is achieved easily by the following code:

```
messageService.RegisterHandler<HelloResponse>(message =>
{
  var helloResponse = message.GetBody();
  helloResponse.Result.Print();

  return null;
});
```

To finish this example, we need a producer of `Hello` objects.

```
var messageProducer =
  inMemoryTransientMessageFactory.CreateMessageProducer();
for (var i = 0; i < 10; i++)
{
  var hello = new Hello
  {
    Name = i.ToString()
  };
  messageProducer.Publish(hello);
}
```

This will generate ten `Hello` objects and publish them on the broker.

What about the exceptions during the execution of a message? This is easily handled by retrying the processing of the message.

```
messageService.RegisterHandler<Hello>(message =>
{
  if (message.RetryAttempts == 0)
  {
    throw new System.Exception();
  }
  var hello = message.GetBody();
  var name = hello.Name;
  var helloResponse = new HelloResponse
                    {
                      Result = "Hello {0}".Fmt(name)
                    };
  return helloResponse;
});
```

This will throw an exception on the first execution, which will trigger a retry until the pre-defined retry attempts are reached. In this scenario, `InMemoryTransientMessageService` does not provide the possibility to inject a custom counter, but instead uses `DefaultRetryCount` that is pre-defined in the base class `TransientMessageServiceBase`, which is 1.

You can provide an exception processing delegate that will override the default retry handling implemented in `ServiceStack.Messaging.MessageHandler<T>`. `DefaultInExceptionHandler`:

```
messageService.RegisterHandler<Hello>(message =>
{
  // some logic here
},
(messageHandler, message, exception) =>
{
  exception.PrintDump();
  var requeue = ++message.RetryAttempts <
  TransientMessageServiceBase.DefaultRetryCount;
  message.Error = exception.ToResponseStatus();
  messageHandler.MqClient.Nak(message,
                              requeue,
                              exception);
});
```

This gives you a deeper insight into how the requeuing process with Message Queues works and how to intercept this process and roll your own logic. The only important thing is that you need to acknowledge the message negatively to the server with a call to `messageHandler.MqClient.Nak`, which will either put the message back into the in-queue (if retry attempts haven't been exceeded) or the DLQ.

Finally, you can also abort the retry process before attempting by throwing an `UnRetryableMessagingException` object (which can even encapsulate an inner exception) with the default exception handling delegate.

```
messageService.RegisterHandler<Hello>(message =>
{
    throw new
    ServiceStack.Messaging.UnRetryableMessagingException("something
    went terribly wrong");
});
```

RCON

The next step is to message across the process and machine boundaries, which is done by using the RCON service and client. The server and client are located in the `ServiceStack.Server` NuGet package (`ServiceStack.Messaging.Rcon`), as shown here:

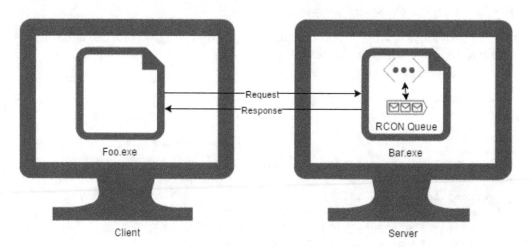

This solution is a bit of an exception though; it neither involves an external broker to which you can assign multiple services, nor a persistence of messages. In fact the process that hosts a `Server` object is the broker, which makes RCON a perfect basis for a direct machine-to-machine communication to implement your own Message Queue. Another important issue with RCON is the non-existent storage of messages, that vanish when the service restarts.

```
using System;
using System.Net;
using ServiceStack;
using ServiceStack.Text;

const int port = 12345;
var ipEndPoint = new IPEndPoint(IPAddress.Any,
                                port);
var server = new ServiceStack.Messaging.Rcon.Server(ipEndPoint);
server.RegisterHandler<Hello>(message =>
{
  var hello = message.GetBody();
  var name = hello.Name;
  var helloResponse = new HelloResponse
  {
    Result = "Hello {0}".Fmt(name)
  };
  return helloResponse;
});
server.Start();
```

This will create a listener on port `12345` on the local machine and register a handler for the incoming `Hello` requests.

To use this server, we will create a client and send a `Hello` object over the wire and handle the response.

```
using System;
using System.Net;
using ServiceStack;
using ServiceStack.Text;

const int port = 12345;
var ipAddress = IPAddress.Loopback;
```

```
var ipEndPoint = new IPEndPoint(ipAddress, port);

var client = new ServiceStack.Messaging.Rcon.Client(ipEndPoint);
client.Connect();

for (var i = 0; i < 10; i++)
{
  var hello = new Hello
  {
    Name = i.ToString()
  };
  client.Call(hello,
              (rconClient,
               response) =>
  {
    var message = response.ToMessage<HelloResponse>();
    var helloResponse = message.GetBody();
    helloResponse.Result.Print();
  });
}
```

This creates a client that sends the requests to the port 12345 on the local machine (in a real-world example you'd have to adapt the ipAddress variable to reflect your server's IP). Compared to the prior example of the *In Memory MQ* section, this solution only provides an explicit and direct communication back to the client, which is reflected by the callback parameter of the client.Call method.

As there's no built-in retry, you will have to adapt the callback parameter to republish the initial DTO if there is a failure.

```
client.Call(hello,
            CallbackAfterHello);

private void CallbackAfterHello(Client client, byte[] response)
{
  var initialMessage = response.ToMessage<Hello>();
  if (initialMessage.Error != null)
  {
    var hello = initialMessage.GetBody();
    client.Call(hello,
                CallbackAfterHello);
  }
```

```
      else
      {
        var message = response.ToMessage<HelloResponse>();
        var helloResponse = message.GetBody();
        helloResponse.Result.Print();
      }
    }
```

The round-trip to the client on exceptions is a deal breaker as you cannot send an IMessage<T> object back to the server, which makes the transferal of the retry attempts impossible. So essentially, on every subsequent client.Call invocation you lose the present retry counter.

To get around this limitation, you can implement your own client, which is capable of sending IMessage<T> objects:

```
    public class Client : ServiceStack.Messaging.Rcon.Client
    {
      private readonly Dictionary<uint, AsyncCallback> _callbacks;

      public Client(IPEndPoint ipEndPoint) : base (ipEndPoint)
      {
        var fieldInfo = typeof (ServiceStack.Messaging.Rcon.Client)
          .GetField("_registeredCallbacks",
                    BindingFlags.Instance | BindingFlags.NonPublic);
        this._callbacks = (Dictionary<uint, AsyncCallback>)
        fieldInfo.GetValue(this);
      }

      public void Call<T>(IMessage<T> message,
                          AsyncCallback callback)
      {
        this._callbacks[this.SequenceID] = callback;
        this.InternalSend(new[]
        {
          Encoding.UTF8.GetBytes(typeof (T).AssemblyQualifiedName),
          message.ToBytes()
        });
      }
    }
```

This derived client has access to the base callbacks via Reflection, which is used to keep the example straightforward. Now we can adapt the `CallbackAfterHello` method.

```
private void CallbackAfterHello(Client rconClient,
                                byte[] response)
{
  var initialMessage = response.ToMessage<Hello>();
  if (initialMessage.Error != null)
  {
    var client = (Client) rconClient;
    client.Call(initialMessage,
                CallbackAfterHello);
  }
  else
  {
    var message = response.ToMessage<HelloResponse>();
    var helloResponse = message.GetBody();
    helloResponse.Result.Print();
  }
}
```

 The internal layout of the sent messages is very versatile and can be found in the internal `ServiceStack.Messaging.Rcon.PacketCodec` class and is worth investigating as it can be the basis for customized messaging implementations over TCP.

RedisMQ

A very basic yet powerful and fully working Message Queue within ServiceStack is RedisMQ, which uses Redis and its features under the hood to implement a persistent queue. The factory and the server are located in the `ServiceStack.Server NuGet` package (`ServiceStack.Messaging.Redis`) and depend on `ServiceStack.Redis` and `ServiceStack.Client` for underlying communication and connection management (`ServiceStack.Redis`).

The components connected to Redis are not generally services or clients but producers and consumers of messages, where a consumer of a message can produce a subsequent message that is consumed by another component, as shown in the following figure:

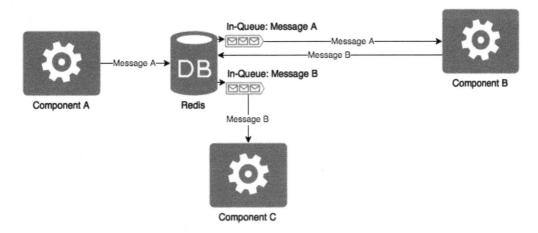

As the underlying technology used is Redis, a certain persistence of the messages is guaranteed (as persistence in Redis can be).

This scenario is easily implemented with the following code (where **Message A** is `Hello` and **Message B** is `HelloResponse`):

```
using System;
using ServiceStack;
using ServiceStack.Messaging.Redis;
using ServiceStack.Redis;
using ServiceStack.Text;

var redisClientManager = new BasicRedisClientManager();
var redisMqServer = new RedisMqServer(redisClientManager);
var messageProducer = redisMqServer.CreateMessageProducer();

var hello = new Hello
{
  Name = "Component A"
};
messageProducer.Publish(hello);
```

This code excerpt from **Component A** creates a `BasicRedisClientManager` instance that is used to create a `RedisMqServer` instance, which is then used to create an `IMessageProducer` instance (`messageProducer`). This instance is then utilized to publish an instance of `Hello` to Redis.

We will proceed with registering a handler for `Hello` instances in **Component B**.

```
using System;
using ServiceStack;
using ServiceStack.Messaging.Redis;
using ServiceStack.Redis;
using ServiceStack.Text;

var redisClientManager = new BasicRedisClientManager();
var redisMqServer = new RedisMqServer(redisClientManager);

redisMqServer.RegisterHandler<Hello>(message =>
{
  var hello = message.GetBody();
  var name = hello.Name;
  var helloResponse = new HelloResponse
  {
    Result = "Hello {0}".Fmt(name)
  };

  return helloResponse;
});
redisMqServer.Start();
```

 Due to simplicity, we use the default parameter-less constructor of a client manager, which connects to a local Redis instance. However, you can provide one or multiple Redis hosts to connect with.

The registered handler for `Hello` objects creates a `HelloResponse` object and returns it back to Redis, in which we will register a handler for **Component C** that prints the content of the `Result` property to the console.

```
using System;
using ServiceStack;
using ServiceStack.Messaging.Redis;
```

```
using ServiceStack.Redis;
using ServiceStack.Text;

var redisClientManager = new BasicRedisClientManager();
var redisMqServer = new RedisMqServer(redisClientManager());

redisMqServer.RegisterHandler<HelloResponse>(message =>
{
  var helloResponse = message.GetBody();
  var result = helloResponse.Result;
  result.Print();

  return null;
});
redisMqServer.Start();
```

As we do not want to return another response to `HelloResponse`, we exit the further process by simply returning `null`.

This basic example shows the strength of RedisMQ by providing all the features of a real Message Queue with a visualized dataflow, the possibility to add more components on the go, and the simplicity of the setup of such a queue.

The default degree of parallelism is 1 but it can be changed by providing a parameter noOfThreads to a `RegisterHandler` call:

```
redisMqServer.RegisterHandler<T>(message => {}, 2);
```

Setup

The setup of RedisMQ is quite simple. All you need to do is to grab and install the release of Redis from `http://redis.io/download` (or `https://github.com/MSOpenTech/redis/releases` for Windows releases) on the machine, which will host the broker. Once the setup is completed, you will have a running instance of Redis available, which can interact with the RedisMQ package from ServiceStack.

Client managers

The first object we need to create is a `RedisMqServer` object, it's a client manager that is responsible for the creation of an `IRedisClient` object, which is used to communicate with Redis. The only shipped implementation of this writing is `ServiceStack.Redis.RedisClient`; however, you can simply roll your own client manager by implementing the `IRedisClientsManager` interface.

The following client managers are available for the creation of `IRedisClient` objects:

- `ServiceStack.Redis.BasicRedisClientManager`: This client manager returns a new client on every client retrieval call, which makes the returned clients implicitly thread-safe. As this client manager also implements `ServiceStack.Redis.IRedisFailover` there's a possibility to use multiple endpoints for normal and read-only clients, which get iterated by round robin. You can provide a different endpoint for read-only clients if you do not need a failover handling, which will use the normal (read and write) endpoint for creation.

- `ServiceStack.Redis.PooledRedisClientManager`: A reuse of clients is added, in contrast to the prior `BasicRedisClientManager`. The clients are retrieved in a thread-safe and round robin manner. You can supply the timeout for the retrieval of clients with `PoolTimeout` or `RecheckPoolAfterMs`. If the maximum pool size is reached an exception is thrown according to the mentioned timeout.

- `ServiceStack.Redis.RedisManagerPool`: This is the successor of `PooledRedisClientManager` with the ability to spawn clients even if the maximum pool size is reached by maintaining the instances outside of the pool.

- `ServiceStack.Redis.Support.Diagnostic.TrackingRedisClientManager`: This client manager is a wrapper for the other client managers and provides logging of the client allocations. As well as tracking the creation and disposal of client instances, every 30 seconds the current state of the manager is published to a `log4net` logger, named `ServiceStack.Redis.Support.Diagnostic.TrackingRedisClientsManager`.

All client managers share the following common properties to set timeouts:

- `ConnectTimeout`
- `SocketSendTimeout`
- `SocketReceiveTimeout`
- `IdleTimeOutSecs`

You can use the common `RedisClientFactory` property for the injection of a client factory.

Queues

The generation of queue names is implemented in `ServiceStack.Messaging.QueueNames`, where all the basic prefixes reside along with the `ResolveQueueNameFn` delegate, which can be overridden at any time. The base name is then suffixed with the corresponding queue type.

For RedisMQ the following queue types exist:

- **In** (default `mq:{type}:inq`): This is the initial queue, messages get passed in and taken out in "first come first serve" order.

- **Out** (default `mq:{type}:outq`): This queue stores all the successfully processed messages with a default limit of 100 entries.

  You can avoid storing the successfully processed messages in the out-queue by simply setting the `Options` property of the incoming message in your handler accordingly.

  ```
  redisMqServer.RegisterHandler<Hello>(message =>
  {
    message.Options = (int) MessageOptions.None;
    return null;
  });
  ```

- **Dead letter queue** (default `mq:{type}:dlq`): This queue is responsible to store all the messages, whose processing has failed and exceeded the retry counter. You can subscribe to this queue to trigger a re-enqueuing or reporting.

You can get messages from the DLQ by simply using `QueueNames<T>`. `Dlq` as the `queueName` parameter of an `IMessageQueueClient`. `Get<T>` call. The messages stored in this queue also contain the last exception that caused the storing in the DLQ on the `Error` property.

- **Priority** (default `mq:{type}:priorityq`): This queue is a separate in-queue to which you can register in order to map a priority scenario.

Even though the priority is mapped with a `long` property on the messages, RedisMQ makes no difference between any priority that is greater than `0`. Giving more priority to messages with a higher priority level is a feature of other Message Queue solutions.

Replying directly back to the producer

The usual delivery chain of Message Queues is based on a "first come, first serve" principle for any registered handler. This means that if there's a response to a message, it is not guaranteed that the ensuing receiver of the response will be the original sender of the request.

To get over this limitation there's a pattern for your rescue, which uses a temporary queue whose name is added to the initial request.

```
using ServiceStack.Messaging;

var messageQueueClient = redisMqServer.CreateMessageQueueClient();

var hello = new Hello
{
  Name = "reply to originator"
};
var queueName = messageQueueClient.GetTempQueueName();
var message = new Message<Hello>(hello)
{
  ReplyTo = queueName
};
messageProducer.Publish(hello);
var response = messageQueueClient.Get<HelloResponse>(queueName);
var helloResponse = response.GetBody();
```

This will create a temporary queue (that follows the default pattern of `mq:temp:{guid}`) that is assigned to the `ReplyTo` property of the newly introduced message, which encapsulates a `Hello` object. To read from this temporary queue we need to use a queue client instead of a message producer that is achieved by using the return value of `CreateMessageQueueClient`. The call to `Get` is blocked and will not resume until a message is retrieved from the temporary queue. You can also use `GetAsync`, it isn't fully asynchronous but will return `null` if there's no message in the queue, which makes calling it inevitable within a `while` construct.

The nature of this queue is temporary and it gets deleted after a message is retrieved from it.

> The action that should be applied according to the `ReplyTo` value is determined by `ServiceStack.ClientFactory.Create`. It gives you the possibility to use a URI instead of a queue name to post the return value to the given URI.

Integrate a RedisMQ client into your service

Adding RedisMQ to your system doesn't mean that you are stuck with a Redis context, you can also expose the handler via a ServiceStack service.

First, you need to implement the handler of `Hello` on a service:

```
using ServiceStack;

public class Service : ServiceStack.Service,
                       IAny<Hello>
{
  public object Any(Hello request)
  {
    var name = request.Name;
    var helloResponse = new HelloResponse
    {
      Result = "Hello {0}".Fmt(name)
    };
    return helloResponse;
  }
}
```

This defines a service class with a handler that is reachable over HTTP.

Next, we need to create a host to encapsulate our newly created service:

```
using Funq;
using ServiceStack;
using ServiceStack.Messaging.Redis;
using ServiceStack.Redis;

public class AppHost : AppSelfHostBase
{
  public AppHost()
    : base ("Hello Service", typeof (Service).Assembly) {}

  public override void Configure(Container container)
  {
    this.Routes.Add<Hello>("/hello");
    this.Routes.Add<Hello>("/hello/{Name}");

    container.Register<IRedisClientsManager>(arg => new
    RedisManagerPool());
    var redisClientsManager =
    container.Resolve<IRedisClientsManager>();
    var redisMqServer = new RedisMqServer(redisClientsManager);
    redisMqServer.RegisterHandler<Hello>
    (this.ServiceController.ExecuteMessage);
    redisMqServer.Start();
  }
}
```

This creates a host we can start in our component, it holds a service that listens to Hello requests over HTTP and Redis.

We can even extend this example to publish messages in our service handlers to RedisMQ by utilizing the Publish method of services, as shown here:

```
public void Any(...)
{
  var hello = new Hello
  {
    Name = "Foobar";
  };
  this.Publish(hello);
}
```

To make this work we need to register a `ServiceStack.Messaging.`
`IMessageFactory` mapping in our `IoC` container:

```
public override void Configure(Funq.Container container)
{
  container.Register<IRedisClientsManager>(arg => new
  RedisManagerPool());
  container.RegisterAs<RedisMessageFactory, IMessageFactory>();
}
```

 For further optimization you can increase the scope of the registration of `RedisMessageFactory` to the lifetime of the application (singleton).

RabbitMQ

RabbitMQ is a mature broker built on top of the **Advanced Message Queuing Protocol (AMQP)**, which makes it possible to solve even more complex scenarios, as shown here:

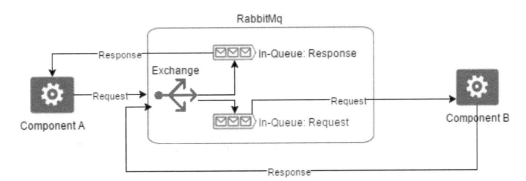

The messages will survive restarts of the RabbitMQ service and the additional guarantee of delivery is accomplished by depending on an acknowledgement of the receipt (and processing) of the message, by default this is done by ServiceStack for typical scenarios.

The client of this Message Queue is located in the `ServiceStack.RabbitMq` NuGet package (it uses the official client in the `RabbitMQ.Client` package under the hood).

You can add additional protocols to RabbitMQ, such as **Message Queue Telemetry Transport (MQTT)** and **Streaming Text Oriented Messaging Protocol (STOMP)**, with plugins to ease Interop scenarios.

Due to its complexity, we will focus on an abstracted interaction with the broker. There are many books and articles available for a deeper understanding of RabbitMQ. A quick overview of the covered scenarios is available at `https://www.rabbitmq.com/getstarted.html`.

The method for publishing a message with RabbitMQ does not differ much from RedisMQ:

```
using ServiceStack;
using ServiceStack.RabbitMq;

using (var rabbitMqServer = new RabbitMqServer())
{
  using (var messageProducer =
  rabbitMqServer.CreateMessageProducer())
  {
    var hello = new Hello
    {
      Name = "Demo"
    };
    messageProducer.Publish(hello);
  }
}
```

This will create a `Hello` object and publish it to the corresponding queue in RabbitMQ. To retrieve this message, we need to register a handler, as shown here:

```
using System;
using ServiceStack;
using ServiceStack.RabbitMq;
using ServiceStack.Text;

var rabbitMqServer = new RabbitMqServer();
rabbitMqServer.RegisterHandler<Hello>(message =>
{
```

```
    var hello = message.GetBody();
    var name = hello.Name;
    var result = "Hello {0}".Fmt(name);

    result.Print();

    return null;
});
rabbitMqServer.Start();


"Listening for hello messages".Print();

Console.ReadLine();

rabbitMqServer.Dispose();
```

This registers a handler for `Hello` objects and prints a message to the console.

> In favor of a straightforward example we are omitting all
> the parameters with default values of the constructor of
> `RabbitMqServer`, which will connect us to the local instance
> at port `5672`. To change this, you can either provide a
> `connectionString` parameter (and optional credentials) or use a
> `RabbitMqMessageFactory` object to customize the connection.

Setup

Setting up RabbitMQ involves a bit of effort. At first you need to install Erlang from `http://www.erlang.org/download.html`, which is the runtime for RabbitMQ due to its functional and concurrent nature. Then you can grab the installer from `https://www.rabbitmq.com/download.html`, which will set RabbitMQ up and running as a service with a default configuration.

Processing chain

Due to its complexity, the processing chain with any mature Message Queue is different from what you know from RedisMQ. Exchanges are introduced in front of queues to route the messages to their respective queues according to their routing keys:

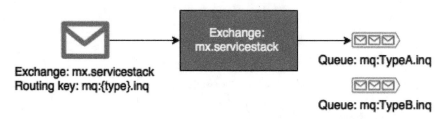

The default exchange name is mx.servicestack (defined in ServiceStack. Messaging.QueueNames.Exchange) and is used in any Publish call of an IMessageProducer or IMessageQueueClient object. With IMessageQueueClient. Publish you can inject a routing key (queueName parameter), to customize the routing of a queue. Failed messages are published to the ServiceStack.Messaging. QueueNames.ExchangeDlq (mx.servicestack.dlq) and routed to queues with the name mq:{type}.dlq. Successful messages are published to ServiceStack. Messaging.QueueNames.ExchangeTopic (mx.servicestack.topic) and routed to the queue mq:{type}.outq. Additionally, there's also a priority queue to the in-queue with the name mq:{type}.priority.

If you interact with RabbitMQ on a lower level, you can directly publish to queues and leave the routing via an exchange out of the picture.

Each queue has features to define whether the queue is durable, deletes itself after the last consumer disconnects, or which exchange is used to publish dead messages with which routing key.

 More information on the concepts, different exchange types, queues, and acknowledging messages can be found at https://www.rabbitmq. com/tutorials/amqp-concepts.html.

Replying directly back to the producer

Messages published to a queue are dequeued in FIFO mode, hence no guarantee
is given that the responses are delivered to the issuer of the initial message.
To force a response to the originator you can make use of the `ReplyTo` property
of a message:

```
using System;
using ServiceStack;
using ServiceStack.Messaging;
using ServiceStack.RabbitMq;
using ServiceStack.Text;

var rabbitMqServer = new RabbitMqServer();
var messageQueueClient =
  rabbitMqServer.CreateMessageQueueClient();

var queueName = messageQueueClient.GetTempQueueName();
var hello = new Hello
{
  Name = "reply to originator"
};
messageQueueClient.Publish(new Message<Hello>(hello)
{
  ReplyTo = queueName
});
var message = messageQueueClient.Get<HelloResponse>(queueName);
var helloResponse = message.GetBody();
```

This code is more or less identical to the RedisMQ approach, but it does something
different under the hood. The `messageQueueClient.GetTempQueueName` object
creates a temporary queue, whose name is generated by `ServiceStack.Messaging.`
`QueueNames.GetTempQueueName`. This temporary queue does not survive a restart of
RabbitMQ, and gets deleted as soon as the consumer disconnects.

 As each queue is a separate Erlang process, you may encounter the
process limits of Erlang and the maximum number of file descriptors
of your OS.

Broadcasting a message

In many scenarios a broadcast to multiple consumers is required, for example if you need to attach multiple loggers to a system it needs a lower level of implementation. The solution to this requirement is to create a fan-out exchange that will forward the message to all the queues instead of one connected queue, where one queue is consumed exclusively by one consumer, as shown:

```
using ServiceStack;
using ServiceStack.Messaging;
using ServiceStack.RabbitMq;

var fanoutExchangeName = string.Concat(QueueNames.Exchange,
                                        ".",
                                       ExchangeType.Fanout);

var rabbitMqServer = new RabbitMqServer();
var messageProducer= (RabbitMqProducer)
  rabbitMqServer.CreateMessageProducer();
var channel = messageProducer.Channel;

channel.ExchangeDeclare(exchange: fanoutExchangeName,
                        type: ExchangeType.Fanout,
                        durable: true,
                        autoDelete: false,
                        arguments: null);
```

With the cast to `RabbitMqProducer` we have access to lower level actions, we need to declare and exchange this with the name `mx.servicestack.fanout`, which is durable and does not get deleted.

Now, we need to bind a temporary and exclusive queue to the exchange:

```
var messageQueueClient = (RabbitMqQueueClient)
  rabbitMqServer.CreateMessageQueueClient();
var queueName = messageQueueClient.GetTempQueueName();
channel.QueueBind(queue: queueName,
                  exchange: fanoutExchangeName,
                  routingKey: QueueNames<Hello>.In);
```

The call to `messageQueueClient.GetTempQueueName()` creates a temporary queue, which lives as long as there is just one consumer connected. This queue is bound to the fan-out exchange with the routing key `mq:Hello.inq`, as shown here:

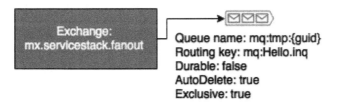

To publish the messages we need to use the `RabbitMqProducer` object (`messageProducer`):

```
var hello = new Hello
{
  Name = "Broadcast"
};
var message = new Message<Hello>(hello);
messageProducer.Publish(queueName: QueueNames<Hello>.In,
                        message: message,
                        exchange: fanoutExchangeName);
```

 Even though the first parameter of `Publish` is named `queueName`, it is propagated as the `routingKey` to the underlying `PublishMessage` method call.

This will publish the message on the newly generated exchange with `mq:Hello.inq` as the routing key:

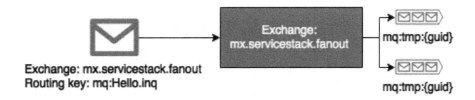

Now, we need to encapsulate the handling of the message as:

```
var messageHandler = new MessageHandler<Hello>(rabbitMqServer,
                                                message =>
{
  var hello = message.GetBody();
  var name = hello.Name;

  name.Print();

  return null;
});
```

The `MessageHandler<T>` class is used internally in all the messaging solutions and looks for retries and replies.

Now, we need to connect the message handler to the queue.

```
using System;
using System.IO;
using System.Threading.Tasks;
using RabbitMQ.Client;
using RabbitMQ.Client.Exceptions;
using ServiceStack.Messaging;
using ServiceStack.RabbitMq;

var consumer = new RabbitMqBasicConsumer(channel);
channel.BasicConsume(queue: queueName,
                     noAck: false,
                     consumer: consumer);

Task.Run(() =>
{
  while (true)
  {
    BasicGetResult basicGetResult;
    try
    {
      basicGetResult = consumer.Queue.Dequeue();
    }
    catch (EndOfStreamException)
    {
      // this is ok
      return;
    }
    catch (OperationInterruptedException)
    {
```

```
    // this is ok
    return;
  }

  var message = basicGetResult.ToMessage<Hello>();
  messageHandler.ProcessMessage(messageQueueClient,
                                message);
  }
});
```

This creates a `RabbitMqBasicConsumer` object, which is used to consume the temporary queue. To process messages we try to dequeue from the `Queue` property in a separate task.

 This example does not handle disconnects and reconnects from the server and does not integrate with the services (however, both can be achieved).

Integrate RabbitMQ into your service

The integration of RabbitMQ in a ServiceStack service does not differ overly from RedisMQ. All you have to do is adapt it to the `Configure` method of your host.

```
using Funq;
using ServiceStack;
using ServiceStack.Messaging;
using ServiceStack.RabbitMq;

public override void Configure(Container container)
{
  container.Register<IMessageService>(arg => new
  RabbitMqServer());
  container.Register<IMessageFactory>(arg => new
  RabbitMqMessageFactory());

  var messageService = container.Resolve<IMessageService>();
  messageService.RegisterHandler<Hello>
  (this.ServiceController.ExecuteMessage);
  messageService.Start();
}
```

The registration of an `IMessageService` is needed for the rerouting of the handlers to your service; and also, the registration of an `IMessageFactory` is relevant if you want to publish a message in your service with `PublishMessage`.

Server-sent events

The web has always been a different playing field from the ground up, leaving no chance to interact with the client once the response is finished. This changed in the early 2000's with the rise of Ajax. Suddenly, the clients could request resources without requesting new HTML page. The next big problem that needed to be solved was the communication from the server to the client, which was done by introducing long polling when the client opened an HTTP request to which the server subsequently responded to, but never closed. This raised several issues but the biggest was the waste of resources by keeping the connection constantly alive. Servers with multiple concurrent users ran out of connections and the idea of keeping a connection open, even when there was no change, was a thorn in developers' flesh.

Some years later, in the early 2010's, RFC 6455 was adopted. Web Sockets, which is a part of the HTML 5 standard got introduced to the public but suffered from a slow implementation in all browsers.

Many frameworks have popped up on the radar, simplifying the integration of pushes from the server by cleverly deciding the used parameters of a bidirectional connection. The best known framework of this kind for the .NET developers is **SignalR**.

An alternative technology that ServiceStack ships a client and provider for is **server-sent events,** which works on top of the EventSource class in HTML 5.

 All the major browsers are supported, yet IE makes an exception here. Nevertheless, there's a polyfill solution that brings EventSource to IE: http://html5doctor.com/server-sent-events/#yaffle.

First, we will create a Razor view to show you the essential stuff on the client:

```
@{
    var serverEventsFeature = this.GetPlugin<ServerEventsFeature>();
}
<script src="/Scripts/jquery-2.1.4.min.js"></script>
<script src="/js/ss-utils.js"></script>
<script type="text/javascript">
    var eventSource = new
    EventSource('@serverEventsFeature.StreamPath?t=' + new
    Date().getTime());
    $(eventSource).handleServerEvents({
        handlers: {
```

```
    Say: function (msg) {
        console.log(msg);
    }
  }
 }
});
</script>
```

You need to include jQuery and the ominous `ss-utils.js`, to give you access to all the bundled resources of ServiceStack.

 If you decide to go for a web form implementation and host the service under a different location, you need to adapt the source of `ss-utils.js` as well, as it gets served by the ServiceStack handler.

An `EventSource` object is created and with the help of jQuery, an event handler is bound to the `Say` event. At this stage we do nothing more than logging the message to the console.

Now we set up the server side, as shown here:

```
public class Say
{
    public string Message { get; set; }
}
```

The `Say` class is our DTO, which we will send from the server to the client.

Now, we need to set up our host and add several features to it. The most important one is `ServerEventsFeature`. It is set up as follows:

```
using Funq;
using ServiceStack;
using ServiceStack.Razor;

public class AppHost : AppHostBase
{
    public AppHost()
        : base ("Say Service", typeof (AppHost).Assembly) {}

    public override void Configure(Container container)
    {
```

```
        this.Plugins.Add(new RazorFormat());
        this.Plugins.Add(new CorsFeature());
        this.Plugins.Add(new ServerEventsFeature());
    }
}
```

 In order to have a `RazorFormat` available, you need to install the `ServiceStack.Razor` package.

Next, we need to create a service that routes incoming requests to the clients:

```
using ServiceStack;

public class MessageService : Service,
                              IAnyVoid<Say>
{
  public IServerEvents ServerEvents { get; set; }

  public void Any(Say request)
  {
    this.ServerEvents.NotifyAll(request);
  }
}
```

The service class gets auto wired by the IoC-container, so we can use the `ServerEvents` property to forward the messages.

 I left out the configuration of the `web.config` and the instantiation of `AppHost` on purpose, as this is just the plumbing code. You can find the needed adaptions in the code examples.

If you now start up the project, a browser window will open and show you an empty page. You should now open the console with *F12*, and do the following request with cURL:

```
curl http://localhost:54392/json/oneway/Say -X POST -d
  "{\"Message\":\"Hello\"}" -H "Content-Type: application/json"
```

It will result in the following output in your browser's console:

```
        Object {Message: "Hello"}
    > |
```

If you experience a buffered sending of your server events to the client, you need to turn of the compression in your `web.config` or switch to the **Visual Studio Development Server**:

```
<system.webServer>
<urlCompression doStaticCompression="false"
                doDynamicCompression="false"
</system.webServer>
```

Sending messages from the server

There are two ways of interacting with the connected clients; you can either publish to them based on their subscription (channel affine, subscription id and so on) or take advantage of the deep authentication integration.

- `NotifyAll(message)`
- `NotifyAll(selector, message)`
- `NotifyChannel(channel, message)`
- `NotifyChannel(channel, selector, message)`
- `NotifySubscription(subscriptionId, message, channel = null)`
- `NotifySubscription(subscriptionId, selector, message, channel = null)`
- `NotifySession(sspid, message, channel = null)`
- `NotifySession(sspid, selector, message, channel = null)`
- `NotifyUser(userId, message, channel = null)`
- `NotifyUser(userId, selector, message, channel = null)`
- `NotifyUserName(userName, message, channel = null)`
- `NotifyUserName(userName, selector, message, channel = null)`

 Publishing based on the authentication is mainly used when one user can have multiple browser windows or console instances open at the same time. You otherwise would need to gather all the subscription Ids that correspond to a single user (or session) in the same browser instance.

Hooks at the client-side

In this section, we will cover all available possibilities to hook to events provided on the client-side and how to send messages to the server-side.

Subscription events

To build a robust flow on your website you will need several events to determine the current connection state on the client-side. You can extend the `handler` object with the following properties:

- `onConnect: function (subscription, messageEvent)`
- `onJoin: function (subscription, messageEvent)`
- `onHeartbeat: function (subscription, messageEvent)`
- `onLeave: function (subscription, messageEvent)`

The class for `subscription` is `ServiceStack.SubscriptionInfo`, which holds the following properties:

- `CreatedAt:DateTime`
- `Channels:string[]`
- `UserId:string`
- `UserName:string`
- `DisplayName:string`
- `SessionId:string`
- `SubscriptionId:string`
- `UserAddress:string`
- `IsAuthenticated:bool`
- `Meta:Dictionary<string, string>`
- `ConnectArgs:Dictionary<string, string>`

The class for `messageEvent` is `ServiceStack.ServerEventMessage` with the following layout:

- `EventId:long`
- `Channel:string`
- `Data:string`

- `Selector:string`
- `Json:string`
- `Op:string`
- `Target:string`
- `CssSelector:string`
- `Meta:Dictionary<string, string>`

Receiving messages

Additionally, the following global event handler can be attached to the object you pass to `handleServerEvents`, as shown here:

```
success: function (selector, msg, json)
```

This event handler gets called after every message and gives you the changes to do, for example: additional logging.

In contrast to the global `handlers` object you can also go for the `receivers` objects, which map in the following way:

```
messageEvent.data = "{selector}.{target} {msg}"

$(eventSource).handleServerEvents({
  handlers: {
    {target}: function ({msg}) {
      // logic here
    }
  },
  receivers: {
    {selector}: {
      {target}: function ({msg}) {
        // logic here
      }
    }
  }
});
```

> You can further incorporate jQuery events to your website by adding jQuery selectors to your target, which gives you the possibility to route events without any plumbing code.

Sending messages

There's no built-in way to send messages from the client to the server, hence the name. But you can use a regular ServiceStack REST service to send messages to the server, for example with $.post.

Server-side usage of server-sent events

Besides the client-side usage of SSE, you can also use ServiceStack to add push to server-side components. In this section, we will explore how to receive and send messages from a .NET component.

Receiving messages

You can also connect to your server-sent events enabled services with a .NET client. To do so, you need to initialize a ServiceStack.ServerEventsClient object (ServiceStack.Client NuGet package):

```
using ServiceStack;
using ServiceStack.Text;

var serverEventsClient = new ServerEventsClient("http://
localhost:54392");
serverEventsClient.OnMessage = serverEventMessage => {};
serverEventsClient.OnCommand = serverEventMessage => {};
serverEventsClient.OnConnect = serverEventConnect => {};
serverEventsClient.OnException = exception => {};
serverEventsClient.OnHeartbeat = () => {};
serverEventsClient.Connect();
```

The following generic callbacks are available:

- OnMessage: Is fired when there's a message received. The type resides in Target property and the stringified message in the Json property.

- OnCommand: It either receives a ServerEventLeave or ServerEventJoin object.

- OnConnect: It receives a ServerEventJoin object.

- OnException: It receives the exception that occurred on the server.

- OnHeartbeat: It's triggered when there's a heartbeat issued.

Especially, for message processing, a complex handler that captures all types in
`OnMessage` is stressful; however, you can register specific handlers for known targets
with the following code:

```
using System.Collections.Generic;
using ServiceStack;

serverEventsClient.RegisterHandlers(new Dictionary<string,
  ServerEventCallback>
{
  {
    "Say",
    (client, message) =>
    {
      var say = message.Json.FromJson<Say>();
      say.PrintDump();
    }
  }
});
```

To further separate your code you can create a receiver, which works very much like
a service, to avoid the deserialization process on your side and break the code up in a
more logical way.

```
using ServiceStack;
using ServiceStack.Text;

public class CustomReceiver : ServerEventReceiver
{
  public void Say(Say say)
  {
    say.PrintDump();
  }
}
```

The `CustomReceiver` class now gets registered in our `serverEventsClient`:

```
serverEventsClient.RegisterReceiver<CustomReceiver>();
```

You can also register the receiver with `RegisterNamedReceiver<T>(receiverNa
me)` to process messages for a named receiver.

Messages to a specific receiver are sent by convention to the `cmd.{Type}` receiver, so essentially, `RegisterReceiver<T>` calls `RegisterNamedReceiver<T>("cmd")` internally.

Each processing creates a new receiver by default (`NewInstanceResolver` is used as the default instance resolving strategy), unless you either use `SingletonInstanceResolver` or roll your own IoC usage (`Funq` implements `IResolver`, so it can be used directly if you want to):

```
serverEventsClient.Resolver = new SingletonInstanceResolver();
```

Sending messages

Sending messages from a .NET client to the server is achieved by leveraging the `ServiceClient` property.

The following HTTP verb affine methods are available to send messages:

- `{Verb}`: Either returns `void` or the type that is defined on the DTO via `IReturn<T>`.
- `{Verb}Async`: Shows the same behavior as the upper method, but it encapsulates the retrieval in a `Task` object, so you can use `await` to do asynchronous processing that can be cancelled by calling `CancelAsync`.

To complete the interaction options, there are the following HTTP verb agnostic methods available (with their Async-suffixed counterparts that can be cancelled with `CancelAsync`):

- `Send(IReturnVoid)`
- `Send<TResponse>(IReturn<TResponse>)`
- `Send<TResponse>(object)`
- `SendAll<List<TResponse>>(IEnumerable<IReturn<TResponse>>)`
- `SendAllOneWay(IEnumerable<object>)`
- `SendOneWay(object)`
- `SendOneWay(string, object)`

Configure ServerEventsFeature

You have the following options upon the creation of `ServerEventsFeature`:

- Heartbeat settings:
  - `HearbeatInterval`
  - `IdleTimeout`: It's the timeout after which a subscription expires, if no heartbeat occurs
- `LimitToAuthenticatedUsers`
- `NotifyChannelOfSubscriptions`: It defines if the clients should receive a `cmd.onJoin` or `cmd.onLeave` message, if the subscription state of a connected client changes
- Events:
  - `OnConnect`
  - `OnCreated`
  - `OnHeartbeatInit`
  - `OnInit`
  - `OnPublish`
  - `OnSubscribe`
  - `OnUnsubscribe`
- Paths:
  - `HeartbeatPath`
  - `StreamPath`
  - `SubscribersPath`
  - `UnRegisterPath`
  - `ValidateUserAddress`: Only the associated host address can access the subscription. This is checked on any heartbeat or unregister action.

Redis server events

To take the server events a step further, especially if you plan to scale your website by adding more instances and load balancing requests to it, you are confronted with a dilemma, as the subscriptions are not in a shared register. To get around this limitation, there's a drop-in replacement available that leverages Redis as a shared register. The only thing you have to adapt is the `Configure` method of your host:

```
using Funq;
using ServiceStack;
using ServiceStack.Redis;

public override void Configure(Container container)
{
  container.Register<IRedisClientsManager>(arg => new
  RedisManagerPool());
  container.Register<IServerEvents>(arg => new
  RedisServerEvents(arg.Resolve<IRedisClientsManager>()));

  container.Resolve<IServerEvents>().Start();
}
```

Look left and right

Additionally, apart from the basic usage of the introduced Message Queues, you can further advance the implementations, which is reflected in this final section.

Authentication

While taking advantage of the ServiceStack ecosystem and decorating a handler with the `AuthenticateAttribute` attribute, you can only inject credentials along an HTTP request. Thinking outside the box is the key for solving this issue. We are going to use the thinking from *Chapter 2, ServiceStack as Your Unique Point of Access* of the section *Adding authentication and authorization to the Ticket application,* by creating a session in the producer and attaching the session identifier to the DTO, which will then be used in the service to map it to a header based authentication.

First, we need to introduce `SessionId` to our `Hello` DTO.

```
using ServiceStack;

public class Hello : IReturnVoid
                     IHasSessionId
```

```
{
  public string SessionId { get; set; }
}
```

Next, we will adapt our producer to create a permanent session before sending the DTO to our MQ.

```
using ServiceStack;

AuthenticateResponse authenticateResponse;
using (var jsonServiceClient = new
  JsonServiceClient("http://localhost:1337/"))
{
  authenticateResponse = jsonServiceClient.Post(new Authenticate
  {
    RememberMe = true,
    UserName = "johndoe",
    Password = "password"
  });
}
```

To make this Authenticate request succeed, we need to adapt the feature registration of our consumer, as follows:

```
using Funq;
using ServiceStack.Auth;

public override void Configure(Container container)
{
  this.Plugins.Add(new AuthFeature(() => new AuthUserSession(),
                          new IAuthProvider[]
                          {
                              new CredentialsAuthProvider(),
                              new BasicAuthProvider()
                          }));
}
```

This will allow the consumer to expect the Authenticate object as a post payload instead of a basic authentication challenge.

 The setup of an IAuthRepository can be found in *Chapter 2, ServiceStack as Your Unique Point of Access.*

We can now apply the `SessionId` of `authenticateResponse` to our DTO and send it to the MQ, as shown:

```
var hello = new Hello
{
  SessionId = authenticateResponse.SessionId
};
messageQueueClient.Publish(hello);
```

To map the `SessionId` to the headers, we need to adapt our `RegisterHandler` call in our consumer.

```
using ServiceStack;
using ServiceStack.Host;
using ServiceStack.Messaging;
using ServiceStack.Messaging.Redis;
using ServiceStack.Redis;
using Funq;

public override void Configure(Container container)
{
  container.Register<IRedisClientsManager>(arg => new
  RedisManagerPool());

  var redisClientsManager =
  container.Resolve<IRedisClientsManager>();
  var redisMqServer = new RedisMqServer(redisClientsManager);
  redisMqServer.RegisterHandler<Hello>(message =>
  {
    var basicRequest = new BasicRequest
    {
      Verb = HttpMethods.Post
    };
    basicRequest.Headers.Set("X-" + SessionFeature.SessionId,
                             message.GetBody().SessionId);

    var response = this.ServiceController.ExecuteMessage(message,
    basicRequest);

    return response;
  });

  container.Register<IMessageService>(redisMqServer);
}
```

We can now decorate the handler in our service and output a welcome message for the authenticated user.

```
using ServiceStack;
using ServiceStack.Text;

public class Service : ServiceStack.Service,
                       IAnyVoid<Hello>
{
  [Authenticate]
  public void Any(Hello request)
  {
    var session = this.GetSession();
    var name = "{0} {1}".Fmt(session.FirstName,
                             session.LastName);
    var result = "Hello {0}!".Fmt(name);

    result.Print();
  }
}
```

Doing a request in our producer will give us the following console output on the consumer:

Hello John Doe!

The elegance of this approach is that it is totally agnostic to the used Message Queue, as it persists `SessionId` on the DTO, which makes it another decoupled component in our arsenal.

 To get rid of all the boilerplate code that maps the `SessionId` to the headers, you can register a global handler, that injects the value of the `SessionId` property to the headers, if the DTO is implementing the `IHasSessionId` interface.

Filtering requests and responses

Every Message Queue has its own hooks for the purpose of filtering, but ServiceStack offers a centralized hook, which was introduced in *Chapter 1, Distributed Systems and How ServiceStack Jumps in* that is implements simply by leveraging the filtering engine, which is a part of the ServiceStack processing chain.

You simply need to introduce the filters in your `Configure` method, as shown:

```
public override void Configure(Funq.Container container)
{
  this.RegisterTypedMessageRequestFilter<Hello>(
  (request, response, dto) =>
  {
    "Request coming in".Print();
  });
  this.RegisterTypedMessageResponseFilter<HelloResponse>(
  (request, response, dto) =>
  {
    "Request going out".Print();
  });
}
```

This only applies to requests and responses that are directly connected to the Message Queue (hence, the name `RegisterTypedMessageRequest...`). If you offer an HTTP endpoint for the handlers as well, you will have to register filters with `RegisterTypedRequestFilter` and `RegisterTypedResponseFilter` to cover this route as well.

If you do not want to provide an HTTP endpoint, you should use `ServiceStack.Testing.BasicAppHost` to take advantage of the internals of ServiceStack (as mentioned in *Chapter 1, Distributed Systems and How ServiceStack jumps in*).

If you do not plan to integrate your Message Queue into a ServiceStack service you have to go for the filtering hooks provided in the factory and server classes.

Statistics

The `ServiceStack.Messaging.IMessageService` object defines helpful methods to acquire statistics and status information of the used Message Queue. Some statistics and status methods are as follows:

- `GetStats`: Returns a summary of total messages received, processed, retried, and failed
- `GetStatusDescription`: It returns a stringified version of `GetStats`
- `GetStatus`: It returns a string representation of the connection, which can either be `Disposed`, `Stopped`, `Stopping`, `Starting`, or `Started`.

Additionally, there are other options for further details. They are as follows:

- **RedisMQ**:
  - ○ WorkerThreadStatus: It returns a stringified status of each worker thread. Note that, the RedisMQ spawns two threads per registered handler (one for inq and one for priorityq)

- **RabbitMQ**: To get a deeper insight in the performance of RabbitMQ you should install the management tool via the command line and browse http://localhost:15762/:

  rabbitmq/sbin/rabbitmq-plugins enable rabbitmq_management

  rabbitmq/sbin/rabbitmq-service stop

  rabbitmq/sbin/rabbitmq-service start

 You can get further information on the Management Plugin at https://www.rabbitmq.com/management.html.

Summary

In this chapter the messaging pattern was introduced along with all the available clients of existing Message Queues. We set up various data flow scenarios for each queuing technology. In addition to this, we hacked the available solutions to provide direct replies and broadcasts. Finally, server-sent events were introduced, which reveals the possibility to push messages from the server to the client.

In the next chapter, we will focus on how to analyze and tune distributed systems in various ways, while not locking the system to analyze the bottlenecks.

4
Analyzing and Tuning a Distributed System

Overheard at work: "We care about two things: speed and quality. And the quality we care about is speed" –Brad Abrams

Despite the fact that ServiceStack is built with performance in mind, there are several sources that degrade the performance of a system. The sources that can degrade the performance issues are as follows:

- **Inefficient algorithms**: Poor algorithm affects the execution time with minimal load and becomes an even bigger problem under heavy load, due to maxing out resources.

- **Inefficient access paths**: Queries against data stores are executed in an improvable manner (for example, by adding an index to queried columns).

- **Concurrency issues**: The introduction of concurrency also calls for a synchronized access of shared registers that can make the time spent on synchronization more significant by umpteen competing threads. Another issue in this context are weakly designed synchronization mechanisms that introduce deadlock scenarios.

- **Bottlenecks**: When the requests introduced are more than manageable for a system, it can suffer from bottlenecks at various stages of your stack, such as CPU load, memory pressure, IO latency, and synchronization mechanisms.

Besides these subjects, there are many other low-level sources for performance issues, which tend to be more sophisticated to profile.

An application in a distributed system that is troubled with performance issues is a major concern, as the whole system is affected by the weakest link. Cascaded interferences are tougher to track in distributed systems than within monolithic applications. Degrading performance is a scenario to be expected, which makes the decoupled nature of distributed systems an advantage (multiple failovers can and should be added to the environment). Nevertheless, to face this issue upfront, proactive monitoring of applications should be introduced. Murphy's Law is guaranteed to strike, and reaction time is the most precious phase when encountering performance matters.

> *We should forget about small efficiencies, say about 97% of the time: premature optimization is the root of all evil. Yet we should not pass up any opportunities in that critical 3%. A good programmer will not be lulled into complacency by such reasoning, he will be wise to look carefully at the critical code, but only after that code has been identified. –Donald Knuth*

There is one rule of thumb that should be obeyed at all times when optimizing an application: it has to be measured first. Otherwise, it is not possible to tell with certainty what the bottleneck is until you test it from top to bottom and base your optimizations on a reproducible scenario.

Request logging

One key aspect is the detection of problematic requests in a high load scenario and the ability to reproduce the issues the consumer is facing with the same parameters.

The easiest way to add logging of such requests to your service is to use the request logger:

```
using Funq;
using ServiceStack;

public override void Configure(Container container)
{
    this.Plugins.Add(new RequestLogsFeature());
}
```

You can further customize the log entries by adapting the following properties of the `RequestLogsFeature` object:

- `AtRestPath` (default: `/requestlogs`): The route that exposes the gathered logs.

- `EnableSessionTracking` (default: `false`): If set to `true`, the request's associated `ServiceStack.Auth.IAuthSession` instance is added to the `Session` property of the log entries.

- `EnableRequestBodyTracking` (default: `false`): It adds the raw request body to the `RequestBody` property of log entries to verify deserialization or to get insight into the raw request stream.

- `EnableResponseTracking` (default: `false`): It adds the returned response DTO to the `ResponseDto` property of the log entries, if no error occured.

- `EnableErrorTracking` (default: `true`): If an endpoint returns an exception or a `ServiceStack.Web.IHttpError` object, the response is logged.

- `Capacity` (default: `null`): The capacity of the rolling buffer is defined with the constructor parameter of the logger and can be further altered by adapting the value of the property. The default value is `null`, which equals an infinite queue.

- `RequiredRoles` (default: `[ServiceStack.Configuration.RoleNames. Admin]`): If the service is in release mode, the session's roles are checked against the `RequiredRoles` property. If the session holds the admin role – regardless of the actual `RequiredRoles` – no further checking is done.

- `RequestLogger` (default: `null`): You can inject any custom logger by implementing `ServiceStack.Web.IRequestLogger`. If the `RequestLogger` property is `null` upon registration of the plugin, a new instance of `ServiceStack.Host.InMemoryRollingRequestLogger` is used to store entries.

- `ExcludeRequestDtoTypes` (default: `[ServiceStack.Admin.RequestLogs]`): You can exclude logging of requests based on provided RequestDTOs, which by default applies to the `/requestlogs` requests.

- `HideRequestBodyForRequestDtoTypes` (default: `[ServiceStack.Client. Authenticate, ServiceStack.Client.Register]`): Requests of hidden RequestDTOs are logged but the inclusion of the actual DTO is omitted.

You can also secure your logging route by adding an `AuthenticateAttribute` instance to it, as shown:

```
using Funq;
using ServiceStack;
using ServiceStack.Admin;

public override void Configure(Container container)
{
  this.Plugins.Add(new RequestLogFeature());
  typeof (RequestLogsService)
    .AddAttributes(new AuthenticateAttribute());
}
```

Another viable approach for release mode is to take advantage of the `AdminAuthSecret` property of your configuration (`AppHost.Config`), which you can provide via either HTTP header, query string parameter, form data, or cookie. The key is `authsecret` (compiled in `ServiceStack.Keywords.AuthSecret`), which you have to prefix with `X-Param-Override-` (`ServiceStack.Headers.XParamOverride`) if you go for the HTTP header variant.

The previous code instantiates a new instance of `RequestLogsFeature` and adds it to the plugin chain with its default options. You can then request the collected log entries by browsing `/requestlogs`, which outputs all the collected `ServiceStack.RequestLogEntry` objects in **DEBUG** builds and only by the admins in **RELEASE** builds.

With the default configuration, following properties are populated of `RequestLogEntry` objects:

- `Id`: An incremental identifier, based on the application domain.
- `DateTime`: The timestamp of the logging and not the start of the request (which can be calculated by taking `RequestDuration` into account).
- `HttpMethod`: Either the verb of the request or the overridden value by the `X-Http-Method-Override` header.
- `AbsoluteUri` (for example, `http://localhost:5555/hello/John`): The absolute HTTP path of the request.
- `PathInfo` (for example, `/hello/John`): The part of the URL following the domain information (without query string).

- `RequestDto`: The request DTO supplied via either payload, form-data, query string, or URL (if a REST route is used).

- `FormData`: The data that is stored in the form payload.

- `IpAddress`: Holds the user's host address of the request.

- `ForwardedFor`: This property is populated if any load balancer or proxy is used in the transport chain by taking the value of the `X-Forwarded-For` header. You can find more about this header at `https://en.wikipedia.org/wiki/X-Forwarded-For`.

- `Referer`: This is populated by the `Referer` header.

- `Headers`: All of the HTTP headers of the request.

- `UserAuthId`: The value of the `X-UAId` request item (previously populated by valid authentication or session ID providing) or cookie.

- `SessionId`: The value of `ss-pid` (permanent) or `ss-id` (temporary) – depending on the session lifetime – request item, cookie, or HTTP header (prefixed with `x-`).

- `Items`: A dictionary that holds all the keys and stringified (by a `ToString()` call) item's values.

- `ErrorResponse`: Either the response or a `ResponseStatus` DTO wrapping the occurred exception.

- `RequestDuration`: The duration of the request measured by a `System.Diagnostics.Stopwatch` instance that is stored in the requests's Items collection with the name `_requestDurationStopwatch`.

> You can further narrow down the returned log entries if you post a `ServiceStack.Admin.RequestLogs` object to `/requestlogs`. All possible properties are documented in the output of a plain `/requestlogs` request.
>
> However, the following properties are currently not in use:
> - `EnableResponseTracking`
> - `EnableErrorTracking`
> - `ForwardedFor`
> - `HasResponse`

Using another data store for your request log entries

You can customize the storage of your request logging by injecting a ServiceStack. Web.IRequestLogger implementation in a RequestLogsFeature object.

ServiceStack ships a client for Redis, which is an open source and in-memory data structure store, which you can use as a replacement for the InMemoryRollingRequestLogger object.

```
using Funq;
using ServiceStack;
using ServiceStack.Host;
using ServiceStack.Redis;

public override void Configure(Container container)
{
  container.Register<IRedisClientsManager>(arg => new
  PooledRedisClientManager());

  this.Plugins.Add(new RequestLogsFeature
  {
    RequestLogger = new
    RedisRequestLogger(container.Resolve<IRedisClientsManager>())
  });
}
```

This code injects a ServiceStack.Host.RedisRequestLogger instance in the RequestLogsFeature object by resolving a IRedisClientManager object that is already registered in the IoC container (as shown in *Chapter3, Asynchronous Communication between Components*, in the section *RedisMQ*). The violation of the injection principal of IoC is needed here due to RequestLogsFeature registering its default logger during registration. This makes any prior registration of an IRequestLogger mapping invalid.

As the InMemoryRollingRequestLogger instance holds all the relevant methods for the purpose of logging, such as creating a RequestLogEntry object with CreateEntry and filtering request types with ExcludeRequestType, it is advisable to base a custom logger on this class. A basic architecture should look like the following:

```
using System;
using ServiceStack.Host;
```

```
using ServiceStack.Web;

public class CustomRequestLogger : InMemoryRollingRequestLogger
{
  public override Log(IRequest request,
                      object requestDto,
                      object response,
                      TimeSpan requestDuration)
  {
    var requestType = requestDto?.GetType();

    if (this.ExcludeRequestType(requestType))
    {
      return;
    }

    var requestLogEntry = this.CreateEntry(request,
                                           requestDto,
                                           response,
                                           requestDuration,
                                           requestType);

    // logic
  }

  public override List<RequestLogEntry> GetLatestLogs(int? take)
  {
    // logic
  }
}
```

There is absolutely no need to implement GetLatestLogs if you don't want to serve the /requestlogs endpoint. This is especially valid if you plan on redirecting the log entry to a centralized storage.

Additionally, you can inject items to identify the concrete application in request.Items, as the items get added to the log entry.

Centralizing request logging

Gathering and inspecting the request logs can be quite challenging in a distributed environment with lots of services that reside at many different places. Therefore, the introduction of centralized logging is advisable. One might create a custom request logger that appends the data to a central database, but I strongly advise to decouple services from a centralized store by leveraging messaging, as introduced in *Chapter 3, Asynchronous Communication between Components*:

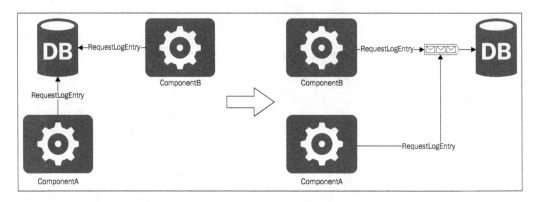

This can be achieved easily with the following logger:

```csharp
using System;
using System.Collections.Generic;
using ServiceStack;
using ServiceStack.Host;
using ServiceStack.Messaging;
using ServiceStack.Web;

public class MessageServiceRequestLogger :
  InMemoryRollingRequestLogger
{
  public MessageServiceRequestLogger(string component)
  {
    this._component = component;
  }

  public IMessageService MessageService { get; set; }

  public override void Log(IRequest request,
```

```
                          object requestDto,
                          object response,
                          TimeSpan RequestDuration)
  {
    var requestType = requestDto?.GetType();

    if (this.ExcludeRequestType(requestType))
    {
      return;
    }

    var requestLogEntry = this.CreateEntry(request,
                                           requestDto,
                                           response,
                                           RequestDuration);

    requestLogEntry.Items.Add("Component", this._component);

    using (var messageProducer =
    this.MessageService.CreateMessageProducer())
    {
      messageProducer.Publish(requestLogEntry);
    }
  }

  public override List<RequestLogEntry> GetLatestLogs(int? take)
  {
    throw new NotImplementedException();
  }
}
```

When the `ServiceStack.Host.ServiceRunner<TRequest>` instance calls the `Log` method of our logger in the `AfterEachRequest` method, the logger uses the injected `IMessageService` object to publish the `RequestLogEntry` object. As this logger simply forwards the messages to the MQ, we can leave out a concrete implementation of the `GetLatestLogs` method.

As mentioned before, the `RequestLogsFeature` object propagates the logger in its `Register` method to the container. This is why we cannot rely on auto-wiring and therefore have to adapt the registration of the feature and its logger.

```
using System;
using Funq;
using ServiceStack;
using ServiceStack.Messaging;
using ServiceStack.RabbitMq;

public override void Configure(Funq.Container container)
{
  container.Register<IMessageService>(arg => new
  RabbitMqServer());

  this.Plugins.Add(new RequestLogsFeature
  {
    RequestLogger = new MessageServiceLogger("Foo Service")
    {
      MessageService = container.Resolve<IMessageService>()
    }
  });
}
```

Tracking requests of your website

Logging the service requests is just half of the story if you host a service within a web application at a designated folder. The following approach works for ASP.NET WebForms as well as for MVC, as the distinction between the request being a service call or a page request is done according to the chosen `HandlerFactoryPath` (which in our example is inferred by the `web.config` file configuration):

```
using System;
using System.Collections.Generic;
using System.Diagnostics;
using System.Web;
using ServiceStack;
using ServiceStack.Web;

public class Global : HttpApplication
{
```

```
private const string StopwatchItemsKey =
"_requestDurationStopwatch";

protected void Application_BeginRequest(object sender,
                                        EventArgs e)
{
  // building a nice apiBasePath to test the FilePath against,
  // which is to determine whether to log or not.
  // something like: /WebSite1/api
  var apiBasePath = string.Concat(this.Request.ApplicationPath,
                                  HostContext.HandlerFactoryPath);
  if (this.Request.FilePath.StartsWith(apiBasePath))
  {
    return;
  }

  // resolving an IRequestLogger instance here assumes
  // a registration, which is accessible by
  // ServiceStack.HostContext.
  var requestLogger = HostContext.TryResolve<IRequestLogger>();
  if (requestLogger != null)
  {
    var stopwatch = Stopwatch.StartNew();
    this.Context.Items[StopwatchItemsKey] = stopwatch;
  }
}
}
```

Whenever a request is initialized, the `FilePath` property of the request is checked against the configured `HandlerFactoryPath` (in a slightly naive way though). If the paths do not match, we inject a new `Stopwatch` instance to `Items` of the request.

Now, we have to introduce a usage of the injected stopwatch, which we implement in the `Application_EndRequest` method, as shown:

```
protected void Application_EndRequest(object src,
                                      EventArgs e)
{
  var stopwatch = (Stopwatch)
  this.Context.Items[StopwatchItemsKey];
  if (stopwatch == null)
  {
```

```
        return;
    }

    stopwatch.Stop();
}
```

The following code adds the logging as highlighted code. This is done by resolving an `IRequestLogger` object from the `HostContext` instance and wrapping the recent native request in an `IRequest` object by calling `TryGetCurrentRequest` on `HostContext`:

```
protected void Application_EndRequest(object src,
                                      EventArgs e)
{
  var stopwatch = (Stopwatch)
  this.Context.Items[StopwatchItemsKey];
  if (stopwatch == null)
  {
    return;
  }

  stopwatch.Stop();

  var requestLogger = HostContext.TryResolve<IRequestLogger>();
  if (requestLogger == null)
  {
    return;
  }

  var request = HostContext.TryGetCurrentRequest();
  if (request == null)
  {
    return;
  }
  requestLogger.Log(request: request,
              requestDto: SerializableQueryString(request.
QueryString),
              response: null,
              elapsed: stopwatch.Elapsed);
}
```

One word of warning: `HostContext.TryGetCurrentRequest` wraps the native request in a decoupled `IRequest` (to be more specific to our scenario: `ServiceStack.Host.AspNet.AspNetRequest`) instance and copies all the items at the very moment of creation. If you add objects to `Items` of the native request afterwards, they don't get copied to the wrapped `IRequest`.

The final step is to implement `SerializableQueryString`, as the `ServiceStack.Web.INameValueCollection` instance cannot be serialized.

```
public static Dictionary<string, string>
  SerializableQueryString(INameValueCollection queryString)
{
  var to = new Dictionary<string, string>(queryString.Count);
  foreach (var key in queryString.AllKeys)
  {
    var value = queryString.Get(key);
    to[key] = value;
  }

  return to;
}
```

Any request to a web page will be logged and can be retrieved by viewing `/api/requestlogs`.

Profiling requests

The next step is to dig deeper into the timings of your service to examine the concrete request and its execution chain. ServiceStack comes with an adapted implementation of MiniProfiler (original implementation available at `http://miniprofiler.com/`), a simple but effective mini-profiler.

Its main goal is to bring profiling to hosted services, but we will implement a solution that works for self-hosted services as well.

To start profiling, we need to adapt the `Application_BeginRequest` method in `Global.asax` file, as shown:

```
using System;
using System.Web;
```

```
using ServiceStack;
using ServiceStack.MiniProfiler;

public partial class Global : HttpApplication
{
  protected void Application_BeginRequest(object sender,
                                          EventArgs e)
  {
    Profiler.Start();
  }
}
```

This starts the profiling for every request (service- and website-requests). You can also limit the profiling to debug mode by verifying the value of `HostContext.Config.DebugMode` or to local request only with `this.Request.IsLocal`.

The profiler needs to be stopped as well, which is done by adapting the `Application_EndRequest` method:

```
public partial class Global : HttpApplication
{
  protected void Application_BeginRequest(object sender,
                                          EventArgs e)
  {
    Profiler.Start();
  }

  protected void Application_EndRequest(object sender,
                                        EventArgs e)
  {
    Profiler.End();
  }
}
```

If you now use a browser to request the JSON report page, you can access the profiling information of the recent requests in the upper right corner of the page, as shown in the following figure:

You can further customize the profiling by adapting the following properties of the `ServiceStack.MiniProfiler.Profiler.Settings` object:

- `ExcludeStackTraceSnippetFromSqlTimings` (default: `false`): It adjusts the rendering of the stack trace to easily find the line with the database call. Disabling this option might improve performance, as no stack trace needs to be gathered.

- `IgnoredPaths` (default: `["/ssr-", "/content", "/scripts", "/favicon.ico"]`): Defines a pattern to disable profiling of certain paths.

- `PopupMaxTracesToShow` (default: `15`): Determines the maximum amount of profiling traces that are shown in the popup.

- `PopupRenderPosition` (default: `ServiceStack.MiniProfiler.Position.Right`): Describes the alignment of the popup.

- `PopupShowTimeWithChildren` (default: `false`): Defines if the time with children should be shown in the popup by default. You can change the visibility by clicking either the **hide time with children** or **show time with children** hyperlink.

- `PopupShowTrivial` (default: `false`): States the initial visibility of steps whose duration were less than `TrivialDurationThresholdMilliseconds`.

- `Results_Authorize`: A delegate to limit to the `/ssr-results` page.

Every profiled request returns the most recent unviewed trace IDs in the `X-MiniProfiler-Ids` HTTP header. You can inspect a specific request and its trace by viewing `/ssr-results?id={id}`, which is relevant if you are making requests outside the scope of the report page and logging the header's result for further examination.

- `ProfilerProvider`: Holds the provider to trace a certain request. The default implantation that is used if no other implementation is injected is `ServiceStack.MiniProfiler.WebRequestProfilerProvider`.

- `ShowControls` (default: `false`): Manages the visibility of the controls to minimize, maximize, or clear the popup.

- `SqlFormatter` (default: `null`): Provides interception of formatting the SQL statement that gets shown in the UI.

- `StackMaxLength` (default: `120`): Defines the maximum length of the embedded stack trace whose embedding is controlled by `ExcludeStackTraceSnippetFromSqlTimings`.

- `Storage` (default: `null`): Represents the storage for the trace entries. If no implementation is injected, then `ServiceStack.MiniProfiler. Storage.HttpRuntimeCacheStorage` is used. You can also use `ServiceStack.MiniProfiler.Storage.SqlServerStorage`, which is available in the `ServiceStack.Server` package.

- `TrivialDurationThresholdMilliseconds` (default: `2.0d`): Defines the upper bound for traces to still qualify as trivial.

- `ExcludeAssembly(assemblyName)`: Excludes all the methods in the given assembly from being added to the stack trace.

- `ExcludeMethod(methodName)`: Excludes a specific method name (without a connection to a specific class) from being added to the stack trace.

- `ExcludeType(typeToExclude)`: Excludes all methods from the given type in the stack trace.

- `LoadVersionFromAssembly()`: Sets the `Version` property of the settings with the MD5 hash of the ServiceStack assembly that is populated with the `ModuleVersionId` of the ServiceStack module by default.

 You can also embed the popup on your WebForms or MVC pages by calling `ServiceStack.MiniProfiler.Profiler. RenderIncludes().AsRaw()`. The `RenderIncludes` method also adds the possibility to override certain settings for a single page.

Profiling self-hosted requests

The default implementation of `ProfilerProvider` (`ServiceStack.MiniProfiler. WebReqeustProfilerProvider`) heavily relies on `System.Web.HttpContext. Current` and cannot be used within a self-hosted scenario. The following custom provider overcomes this limitation by relying on a `ServiceStack.Web.IRequest` object, as shown:

```
using ServiceStack;
using ServiceStack.MiniProfiler;
using ServiceStack.Web;

public partial class CustomProfilerProvider
{
    private const string ProfilerItemsKey = ":mini-profiler:";
    private const string RequestItemsKey = ":request:";
```

```
  private static IRequest GetRequest()
  {
    return (IRequest)
    RequestContext.Instance.Items[RequestItemsKey];
  }

  public static void SetRequest(IRequest request)
  {
    RequestContext.Instance.Items[RequestItemsKey] = request;
  }

  private static Profiler Current
  {
    get
    {
      return (Profiler)
      RequestContext.Instance.Items[ProfilerItemsKey];
    }
    set
    {
      RequestContext.Instance.Items[ProfilerItemsKey] = value;
    }
  }
}
```

This is the base to implement an engine agnostic profiler and needs to be enhanced by implementing the relevant methods of BaseProfilerProvider:

```
using System;
using System.Linq;
using ServiceStack;
using ServiceStack.MiniProfiler;

public partial class CustomProfilerProvider : BaseProfilerProvider
{
  public override Profiler Start(ProfileLevel level)
  {
    var request = GetRequest();
    if (request == null)
    {
      return null;
    }
```

```
    // TODO add probing of request.PathInfo against
    //Settings.IgnoredPaths if needed

    var result = Current = new Profiler(request.AbsoluteUri,
                                        level)
    {
      User = request.RemoteIp,
      Name = path
    };

    SetProfilerActive(result);

    return result;
}

public override void Stop(bool discardResults)
{
    var profiler = Current;
    if (profiler == null)
    {
      return;
    }

    if (!StopProfiler(profiler))
    {
      return;
    }

    if (discardResults)
    {
      Current = null;
      return;
    }

    SaveProfiler(profiler);

    // TODO add "X-MiniProfiler-Ids" HTTP header, to provide a
    // data source to the client-side if needed
}

public override Profiler GetCurrentProfiler()
{
    return Current;
}
}
```

The final two steps in the implementation are the injection of the logger in the settings, and the injection of the request in the logger, which is both done in the `Configure` method:

```
using Funq;
using ServiceStack;
using ServiceStack.MiniProfiler;

public override void Configure(Container container)
{
  // we are not utilizing GlobalRequestFilters here
  // as we need to start before any deserialization happens.
  Profiler.Settings.ProfilerProvider = new
  CustomProfilerProvider();

  this.RawHttpHandlers.Add(request =>
  {
    CustomProfilerProvider.SetRequest(request);

    Profiler.Start();

    return null;
  });

  this.GlobalResponseFilters.Add((request,
                                  response,
                                  dto) =>
  {
    Profiler.Stop();
  });
}
```

Profiling database requests

You can add the timings of the SQL commands to the profiling by simply wrapping the database connection of your `OrmLiteConnectionFactory` with `ServiceStack.MiniProfiler.Data.ProfiledDbConnection`.

```
using Funq;
using ServiceStack;
using ServiceStack.Data;
using ServiceStack.MiniProfiler;
```

```
using ServiceStack.MiniProfiler.Data;
using ServiceStack.OrmLite;

public override void Configure(Container container)
{
  container.Register<IDbConnectionFactory>(arg => new
  OrmLiteConnectionFactory(...)
  {
    ConnectionFilter = dbConnection => new
    ProfiledDbConnection(dbConnection, Profiler.Current)
  });
}
```

Now, inspecting the details of the request gives us information regarding executed statements:

You can then click on the count and inspect all the executed readers, scalar, and non-query commands.

Finally, the profiler comes with an automatic detection of duplicate queries, which makes classic O(n) (or worse) operations quite easy to spot.

In case of detected duplicate queries an exclamation mark is added to the relevant step and you can further identify the commands by clicking on the link and searching for queries with a *DUPLICATE* label.

Adding custom steps for fine-grained profiling

To enable a convenient possibility for a drill-down view, you can make use of custom steps with as many levels as you need.

```
using ServiceStack;
using ServiceStack.MiniProfiler;
```

```
public object Any(Hello request)
{

    using (Profiler.Current.Step("Custom Step"))
    {
      var name = request.Name;
      using (Profiler.StepStatic("Inner custom step"))
      {
        var helloResponse = new HelloResponse
        {
          Result = "Hello {0}".Fmt(name)
        };
        return helloResponse;
      }
    }
}
```

This will result in the following output:

/hello/foo	PC on Thu, 1 Jan 1970, 00:00:00 GMT	
	duration (ms)	from start (ms)
http://localhost:57027/hello/foo	1.8	+0.0
Deserialize Request	0.0	+0.6
Executing Request Filters	0.0	+0.7
Execute Service	0.0	+0.7
Custom Step	0.0	+0.7
Inner custom step	0.0	+0.7
Executing Response Filters	0.0	+0.7
Writing to Response	0.6	+0.7

> You can use either `Profiler.Current.Step` or `Profiler.StepStatic`, both call the same method internally to create blocks.

Alternatively, for simply wrapping small blocks you can use `Profiler.Current.Inline` to trace a delegate with a return value, such as:

```
var helloResponse = Profiler.Current.Inline(() => new
  HelloResponse(), "Inner custom step");
```

Centralizing request profiling

You can centralize the profiled requests with any MQ by using the following implementation, as also shown for centralizing request logging:

```
using System;
using System.Collections.Generic;
using ServiceStack;
using ServiceStack.Messaging;
using ServiceStack.MiniProfiler;
using ServiceStack.MiniProfiler.Storage;

public class MessageServiceStorage : IStorage
{
  public IMessageService MessageService { get; set; }

  public void Save(Profiler profiler)
  {
    using (var messageProducer =
    this.MessageService.CreateMessageProducer())
    {
      messageProducer.Publish(profiler);
    }
  }

  // Loading an GetUniqueViewedIds is defined by
  // the interface, but not needed in our example.
  public Profiler Load(Guid id)
  {
    return null;
  }

  public List<Guid> GetUnviewedIds(string user)
  {
    return new List<Guid>(0);
  }
}
```

This class is a generic approach by leveraging the injected implementation in the `MessageService` property to publish objects.

To use this storage, you need to adapt your host's configuration, as shown:

```
using Funq;
using ServiceStack;
using ServiceStack.Messaging;
using ServiceStack.MiniProfiler;
using ServiceStack.MiniProfiler.Storage;
using ServiceStack.RabbitMq;

public override void Configure(Container container)
{
  container.Register<IMessageService>(arg => new
  RabbitMqServer());
  container.RegisterAutoWiredAs<MessageServiceStorage,
  IStorage>();

  Profiler.Settings.Storage = container.Resolve<IStorage>();
}
```

The custom implementation of `IStorage` gives a deeper understanding of how the profiling works: the `Profiler` object gets saved to a storage after the profiler is stopped and the unviewed object's `Id` is returned to the client according to the `User` property (usually the IP address of the client, unless you customize the settings). On the client-side the browser issues multiple AJAX requests to retrieve the actual objects from the `Load` method back-to-back (which you can also do manually by browsing `/ssr-results?id={id}`).

 Finally, I would like to introduce you to the MiniProfilingToolkit (`https://bitbucket.org/migajek/miniprofilingtoolkit`) by Michał Gajek, a graphical interface for request profiling, which introduces a storage that forwards the objects to a remote service that also holds an interface to browse and analyze the collected requests.

Minimizing the footprint of HTTP requests

One possible approach to minimize the overall demand of resources of a web service is to shrink the HTTP footprint. Each established connection uses valuable resources, which makes a conversion to batching requests a possible solution. Additionally, you can also try to minimize the amount of transmitted data by adding compression or using a more advanced format. However, always keep the additional CPU time needed for compression and advanced serialization in mind, which might excel the benefit of saved transferred bytes.

Batching requests

To further improve performance for classic $O(n)$ operations, implicit auto batching is available with all ServiceStack .NET clients. This minimizes the amount of requests needed, minimizes latency, and also optimizes potential requests to a database (for example, by acquiring only one transaction instead of multiple).

To make use of automatic request batching, you can use any of the SendAll methods available on the client. They are as follows:

```
var jsonServiceClient = new JsonServiceClient();
jsonServiceClient.SendAll(...);
jsonServiceClient.SendAllAsync(...);
jsonServiceClient.SendAllOneWay(...);
```

Batching does not require any additional implementation of the service itself, as the client simply sends the collection to a predefined route: /json/reply|oneway/ {Type}[].

ServiceStack then processes the collection as single calls to the handler internally, and returns the responses in the same order as the requests as one:

```
public class HelloService : IService,
                            IAny<Hello>
{
  public object Any(Hello request)
  {
    return new HelloResponse
    {
      Result = "Hello {0}".Fmt(request.Name);
    };
  }
}
```

```
using (var jsonServiceClient = new JsonServiceClient())
{
  var requests = new []
  {
    new Hello { Name = "Person 1" },
    new Hello { Name = "Person 2" },
    new Hello { Name = "Person 3" }
  };

  var responses = jsonServiceClient.SendAll(requests);
  // outputs
  // Hello Person 1
  // Hello Person 2
  // Hello Person 3
}
```

Customizing automatic batching

In many scenarios, a custom implementation of batching improves the performance further, such as receiving high load over a period of time or mostly by common and natural degradation of performance due to multiple database accesses or transactions.

The simplest approach is to take advantage of the predefined route /json/reply|oneway/{Type}[] and implement the custom handler as:

```
public class HelloService : Service,
                            IAnyVoid<Hello>,
                            IAnyVoid<Hello[]>

{
  public void Any(Hello request)
  {
    this.Db.Insert(request);
  }

  public void Any(Hello[] request)
  {
    this.Db.InsertAll(request);
  }
}
```

This further streamlines the transactions to the database from *n* to 1.

 For example, implementing `IAnyVoid<Hello[]>` does not give any practical usage besides the forced implementation of the method. The handler will, with or without the interface implementation, appear in the metadata page. The return type for `IAny<T[]>` is "incorrectly" stated as void though.

Implementing a RequestDTO to represent a collection

An alternative to automatic batching is to introduce a custom RequestDTO, either representing a collection or holding a collection of elements:

```
public class HelloBatch : List<Hello>,
                          IReturn<HelloResponse[]> {}

public class HelloBatch : IReturn<HelloResponse[]>
{
   public List<Hello> Batch { get; set; }
}
```

These two classes offer a solution to a completely customized batching. They integrate seamlessly into your service similar to other DTO and also show up correctly on the metadata page:

```
public class Service : IService,
                       IAny<HelloBatch>
{
   public object Any(HelloBatch request)
   {
     // implementation
   }
}
```

Compressing requests

The clients of your service can define whether or not they can handle compressed results by injecting supported compression methods in the `Accept-Encoding` HTTP header. The server can choose a method to compress the result from the request HTTP header and then inject the chosen method in the `Content-Encoding` HTTP header and express the actual content type in `Content-Type` of the response.

This "handshake" is implemented in the `ToOptimizedResult` extension method that you can utilize in following ways:

```
using ServiceStack;

public class Service : IService,
                       IAny<Hello>
{
  public object Any(Hello request)
  {
    var helloResponse = new HelloResponse { Result = "Hello
    {0}".Fmt(request.Name) };
    return this.Request.ToOptimizedResult(helloResponse);
  }
}
```

This approach is similar to the usage of `ToOptimizedResultUsingCache`, which was introduced in *Chapter 2, ServiceStack as Your Unique Point of Access*.

You can also enable response compression globally by adapting your host as:

```
using ServiceStack;
using ServiceStack.Web;

public class AppHost : AppSelfHostBase
{
  public override object OnAfterExecute(IRequest req,
                                        object requestDto,
                                        object response)
  {
    response = base.OnAfterExecute(req,
                                   requestDto,
                                   response);

    if (response != null &&
        !(response is CompressedResult))
    {
      response = req.ToOptimizedResult(response);
    }

    return response;
  }
}
```

In fact, you can also create your own `ServiceRunner`, but be warned that due to the late binding of JSONP results, `ServiceStack.CompressedResult` objects are excluded from JSONP wrapping. You can get more information on this topic and a possible workaround at `http://stackoverflow.com/q/19699484`.

Compressing responses

You can also implement request compression by reacting to the compression used in the request, which is reflected by the `Content-Encoding` HTTP header of the request, which is shown in the following code block:

```
using System;
using System.IO;
using System.IO.Compression;
using Funq;
using ServiceStack;
using ServiceStack.Host.AspNet;
using ServiceStack.Host.HttpListener;
using ServiceStack.Web;

public class AppHost : AppSelfHostBase
{
  public override void Configure(Container container)
  {
    this.PreRequestFilters.Add((request, response) =>
    {
      var contentEncoding =
      request.GetHeader(HttpHeaders.ContentEncoding);

      if (string.Equals(contentEncoding,
                        CompressionTypes.GZip,
                        StringComparison.OrdinalIgnoreCase))
      {
        Decompress(request, inputStream =>
        {
          using (var gZipStream = new GZipStream(inputStream,
          CompressionMode.Decompress))
          {
            return new MemoryStream(gZipStream.ToBytes());
          }
        });
      }
    });
  }
}
```

The only chance to intercept the request before any DTO serialization has taken place is a pre-request filter. The filter reads the value of the `Content-Encoding` HTTP header and calls `Decompress` in case the service receives a `gzip` request:

```
public void Decompress(IRequest request,
                       Func<Stream, MemoryStream> decompressFn)
{
  request.UseBufferedStream = true;

  var listenerRequest = request as ListenerRequest;
  var aspNetRequest = request as AspNetRequest;
  if (listenerRequest != null)
  {
    listenerRequest.BufferedStream =
    decompressFn.Invoke(request.InputStream);
  }
  else if (aspNetRequest != null)
  {
    aspNetRequest.BufferedStream =
    decompressFn.Invoke(request.InputStream);
  }
  else
  {
    return;
  }

  request.Headers.Remove(HttpHeaders.ContentEncoding);
}
```

The `Decompress` method sets the `UseBufferedStream` property of the request to `true`, to redirect future access of the stream to the `BufferedStream` property. The resulting decompressed stream is captured by a `MemoryStream` object, which is created by the `decompressFn` delegate. Finally, the HTTP header that is responsible to trigger the decompressing gets removed from the header collection to avoid potential confusion later on in the processing chain.

Alternatively, you can also implement the `IHttpModule` interface to enable request compression in hosted scenarios for the service and pages. You can find more information at http://stackoverflow.com/a/28159849/57508.

Adding MessagePack format

Another solution to minimize the size of requests and responses is to incorporate a binary formatter, such as **MessagePack** (http://msgpack.org/). MessagePack (ServiceStack.MsgPack) can be dropped in and used with your services with a minimum amount of adaptions, as there is no need to annotate your DTOs to allow the usage of the newly introduced format. All you have to do is to register the MsgPackFormat plugin in your host, as shown:

```
using Funq;
using ServiceStack;
using ServiceStack.MsgPack;

public override void Configure(Container container)
{
  this.Plugins.Add(new MsgPackFormat());
}
```

This will make the /x-msgpack/reply|oneway/{Type} endpoint available, which can be used by clients to take advantage of this format.

Clients of your service can use ServiceStack.MsgPack.MsgPackClient with any HTTP verb for requests:

```
using ServiceStack.MsgPack;
using ServiceStack.Text;

using (var msgPackServiceClient = new MsgPackServiceClient(url))
{
  var hello = new Hello
  {
    Name = "John Doe"
  };
  var response = msgPackServiceClient.Post(hello);
}
```

 You can also use REST routes by either injecting Accept HTTP header with application/x-msgpack, or suffixing the URL with either .x-msgpack or ?format=msgpack.

Adding Protobuf format

In contrast to the MessagePack format, the `Protobuf` format, ported by Marc Gravell to .NET, requires additional annotation of your DTOs as the deserialization relies on an order of the members to stay resilient. You can therefore use either `System.Runtime.Serialiation.DataContract` and `System.Runtime.Serialiation.DataMember` attributes, or `Protobuf.ProtoContract` and `Protobuf.ProtoMember`:

```
using System.Runtime.Serialization;
using Protobuf;

[ProtoContract]
[DataContract]
public class Hello : IReturn<HelloResponse>
{
   [ProtoMember(1)]
   [DataMember(Order = 1)]
   public string Name { get; set; }
}
```

 For convenience reasons, you can omit the setting of the `Order` property. The order will then be applied alphabetically. This might not be a good idea regarding the possibility to evolve and version your DTO, as the order is not guaranteed to stay consistent over time.

To integrate this format to your service, you need the NuGet package `ServiceStack.Protobuf`, as well as an adaption of your host:

```
using Funq;
using ServiceStack;
using ServiceStack.ProtoBuf;

public override void Configure(Container container)
{
   this.Plugins.Add(new ProtobufFormat());
}
```

This will make the endpoint `/x-protobuf/reply|oneway/{Type}` available that can be used by clients to take advantage of this format.

Clients can use a `ServiceStack.Protobuf.ProtoBufServiceClient` instance with any HTTP verb for requests.

```
using ServiceStack.ProtoBuf;
using ServiceStack.Text;

using (var protoBufServiceClient= new ProtoBufServiceClient(url))

  var hello = new Hello
  {
    Name = "John Doe"
  };
  var response = protoBufServiceClient.Post(hello);
}
```

> You can also use REST routes by either injecting `Accept` HTTP header with `application/x-protobuf`, or suffixing the URL with either `.x-protobuf` or `?format=protobuf`.

Accessing information provided by RequestInfoFeature

You can gain more insight into your setup appending `?debug=requestinfo` to any of your service routes or by browsing `/requestinfo`. By default, the `RequestInfoFeature` plugin is loaded in debug mode.

The output will give you all relevant information to inspect the loaded plugins, sent headers, embedded resources, and stats of the handlers in the ServiceStack processing chain (registered HTTP handlers, filters, view engines, service types, rest paths, and so on).

The object that gets sent back to the client is of type `ServiceStack.Host.Handlers.RequestInfoResponse`.

Summary

In this chapter, we explored various options to inspect our service and website at runtime, drill down requests by adding custom steps, and improve performance by leveraging batching of requests and database access. Additionally, compression and formats with a smaller footprint were introduced to minimize the impact of request and response size.

In the next chapter, we will discuss the possibilities of make a documentation of your API available and customize the already available metadata page.

5
Documentation and Versioning

One of the most important developments in the last time was the automatic generation of code and documentation to take the burden of manual work and continuous adaptations off developers. Additionally, the asynchronous rollout of features calls for a versioning technique to not break legacy clients of your API.

Metadata page

Adding documentation to your API is a key aspect while creating an understandable and accepted interface. You can roll an automatically generated documentation with your service that ServiceStack populates through annotations on your DTOs. This documentation is generated by the metadata feature (enabled by default) and can be reached by browsing /metadata, which makes the following information available:

1. **A complete list of XML Schema Definition (XSD) types for all services.**

2. A list of all operations excluding the ones that have been hidden by using `[ServiceStack.RestrictAttribute(VisibilityTo = ServiceStack.RequestAttributes.None)]`.

3. Links to all available content formats excluding the ones that have been ignored by your app host's `Config.IgnoreFormatsInMetadata` collection or annotated with `[ServiceStack.RestricitAttribute(VisibilityTo = ServiceStack.RequestAttributes.Any & ~ServiceStack.RequestAttributes.Xml)]`.

4. Links to SOAP 1.1 and 1.2 WSDLs.

5. Links to additional debug information.

You can adapt the base handler path for ServiceStack with `HandlerFactoryPath` of your host's configuration, which also affects the path of the metadata page.

The output of the metadata page looks like the following:

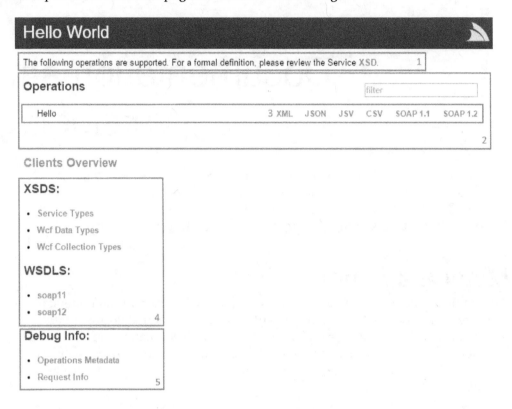

The content is automatically inferred and generated based on the app host's registered and annotated DTOs, which renders an up-to-date document and the possibility for your consumers to interactively explore your API.

You can also disable the documentation by removing it from the features of your app host's configuration, as shown:

```
using ServiceStack;
using Funq;
```

```
public override void Configure(Container container)
{
  this.SetConfig(new HostConfig
  {
    EnableFeatures = Feature.All.Remove(Feature.Metadata)
  });
}
```

Extending the documentation of an operation

The default documentation of an operation gives an excellent, yet basic, overview of the operation's name (1), available routes (2), and involved DTOs (3) with their properties (4):

To override the Content-type in your clients, use the HTTP **Accept** Header, append the **.json** suffix or **?format=json**

To embed the response in a **jsonp** callback, append **?callback=myCallback**

To supplement this documentation, you can add additional attributes to the DTOs, which will be included in the output automatically as:

```
using ServiceStack;

public enum Volume
{
    Normal,
    Loud,
    Gentle
}

[Api("Endpoint to greet a person.")]
[Route("/hello/{Name}", Summary = "Greets a person.", Notes =
    "Longer description")]
public class Hello : IReturn<HelloResponse>
{
    [ApiMember(IsRequired = true, Description =
    "Defines the person to greet.")]
    public string Name { get; set; }

    [ApiMember(IsRequired = true, Description =
    "Defines the volume of the greeting.")]
    [ApiAllowableValues("Volume", typeof (Volume))]
    public Volume Volume { get; set; }
}
```

This code annotates the `Hello` class with an `Api` attribute, which adds a description to the operation's name section. The `Route` attribute adds a summary to the route that provides verb and URL affine descriptions; alternatively, you can also use the `Description` attribute.

The difference between the `Api` and `Description` attributes are quite minimal but the former is more relevant for external test clients, such as **Swagger** (we will discuss this later in the chapter) and the latter does not get exposed to the **Type generator** by default.

You can further limit the documentation of a route, by adding an HTTP verb to the `Route` attribute:

```
[Route("/hello/{Name}", HttpMethods.POST, Summary = "",
    Notes = ""]
```

Additionally, the properties of `Hello` are annotated with `ApiMember` attributes whose information gets added to the DTO section.

When dealing with integer properties, you can use another constructor overload for `ApiAllowableValues`, as shown:

```
[ApiAllowableValues("VolumePercent", 0, 100)
public int VolumePercent { get; set; }
```

You can also provide a fully customized list of values to integer ranges:

```
[ApiAllowableValues("Volume", "Loud", "Gentle",
    "Normal")]
public string Volume { get; set; }
```

The corresponding output of this DTO looks like the following screenshot:

Hello World

<back to all web services

Hello

Endpoint to greet a person.

The following routes are available for this service:

All Verbs	/hello/{Name}	Greets a person.	*Longer description.*

Hello Parameters:

NAME	PARAMETER	DATA TYPE	REQUIRED	DESCRIPTION
Name	path	string	Yes	Defines the person to greet.
Volume	query	Volume	Yes	Defines the volume of the greeting.
				Allowable Values
				• Normal
				• Loud
				• Gentle

 Don't be fooled by the `IsRequired` property of the `ApiMember` attribute, as it is just for documentation reasons. To implement mandatory properties you have to go for a validation, which will be described later in this chapter.

In contrast to adding information to an operation's documentation, you can also remove it by excluding an operation from being output on the metadata page:

```
using ServiceStack;

[Route("/hello/{Name}")]
[Exclude(Feature.Metadata)]
public class Hello : IReturn<HelloResponse>
{
  public string Name { get; set; }
  public Volume Volume { get; set; }
}
```

Finally, you can hide the operations from all features and even from actual execution by annotating your DTO with the `ServiceStack.RestrictAttribute` class. This attribute distinguishes between visibility in the documentation and access for execution by exposing the `VisibleTo` and `AccessTo` property. For easier access, you can also use one of the following properties:

- `VisibleInternalOnly` (adapts `VisibleTo`)
- `VisibleLocalhostOnly` (adapts `VisibleTo`)
- `LocalhostOnly` (adapts `VisibleTo` and `AccessTo`)
- `InternalOnly` (adapts `VisibleTo` and `AccessTo`)
- `ExternalOnly` (adapts `VisibleTo` and `AccessTo`)

 Restricting access works only if the host's configuration `EnableRestrictAccess` property is set to `true` (which is the default).

Configuring the Metadata page

Before you can set a property on a `MetadataFeature` instance, you need to retrieve the registered plugin from the host's configuration with the following code:

```
using Funq;
using ServiceStack;

public override void Configure(Container container)
{
  var metadataFeature = this.GetPlugin<MetadataFeature>();
}
```

The following options are available for customization of the plugin; thus, making it really easy to inject custom links and documentation into the plugin:

- `DebugLinksTitle` (default: `Debug Info:`): This defines the header of the debug section.

- `DebugLinks`: For easier access, you can use the `AddDebugLink` extension method to add custom links to the debug section, which is only shown in debug mode. You can also remove links from this section by calling `RemoveDebugLink` with a URL.

- `PluginLinksTitle` (default: `Plugin Links:`): This defines the header of the plugin links section.

- `PluginLinks`: This stores all the links that get rendered in the plugin links section and is shown when there is at least one plugin link added. For easier access, you can use the `AddPluginLink` extension method build action. You can also remove a link with `RemovePluginLink` by providing the URL.

- `IndexPageFilter`: You can inject a delegate before the index page gets rendered to adapt any of the `ServiceStack.Metadata.IndexOperationsControl` properties.

- `DetailPageFilter`: Similar to `IndexPageFilter`; you can specify a delegate that gets executed before the `ServiceStack.Metadata.OperationControl` gets rendered.

Customizing templates

You can adapt any of the metadata pages with ease, all thanks to the virtual file system that ServiceStack uses, which gives you an easy way to customize resources.

You have the following two options to roll your own pages:

6. Creating an embedded resource with build action *Embedded Resource* that has the name `{Assembly}.Templates.{TemplateName}.html`.

7. Creating a page and copying it with build action *Content* and Copy to the Output Directory *Copy if newer* or *Copy always* to `{output}/Templates/{TemplateName}.html`, which gives you control over the output without the need to recompile your assembly.

The default content of the pages can either be retrieved by resource snooping (for example, with the **Assembly Explorer**) or by browsing the official GitHub repository at `https://github.com/ServiceStack/ServiceStack/tree/master/src/ServiceStack/Templates`.

Customizing the templates is possible to a certain extent only due to the very specific format of the provided placeholders.

One possible solution to integrate custom examples and additional documentation for certain operations could be an additional service, which exposes the extra documentation related to operations. This service can be called and integrated over AJAX from your markup.

HtmlFormat.html

This resource contains the markup for `ServiceStack.Formats.HtmlFormat`, which is used in its `SerializeToStream` method. You can view the page while executing operations through the browser, for example at `http://localhost:5555/hello/Foobar`.

The following placeholders are available:

- `${Dto}`: The response DTO in JSON format
- `${Title}`: `{OperationName} Snapshot of {Timestamp}` for the title tag
- `$(MvcIncludes}`: JavaScript includes for rendering the MiniProfiler (mentioned in *Chapter 4, Analyzing and Tuning a Distributed System*)
- `${Header}`: Similar to `${Title}`, but intended for the h1 HTML tag
- `${ServiceUrl}`: The URL of the operation, which is also used to render the links with a `?format={format}` suffix
- `${Humanize}`: The value of the `ServiceStack.Format.HtmlFormat.Humanize` property, which controls the auto-splitting of "JoinedCase" words

IndexOperations.html

This resource contains the markup for the `ServiceStack.Metadata.IndexOperationsControl` class, which gets rendered when you browse `/metadata`.

The following placeholders are available:

- `{0}`: The title for the `title` HTML tag
- `{1}`: The index of the XSD document that holds all the service types
- `{2}`: The table of all available operations where each row is rendered with the `RenderRow` method
- `{3}`: An unordered list of all available XSD documents

- {4}: The complete markup for the WSDL section
- {5}: An unordered list of all plugin links
- {6}: An unordered list of all debug link

OperationControl.html

This resource contains the markup for the `ServiceStack.Metadata.OperationControl` class, which gets rendered when you browse, for example `/json/metadata?op=Hello`.

The following placeholders are available:

- {0}: The title for the title tag
- {1}: The URL to get back to `/metdata`
- {2}: This is the uppercased content format for the example section's heading `HTML + {ContentFormat}`
- {3}: The operation name
- {4}: This is an example of a request containing relevant HTTP headers and a prepopulated request DTO
- {5}: This is a template of a response containing relevant HTTP headers and a populated response DTO
- {6}: This is HTML snippet contains all the information that is attached with `Api`, `Description`, `Route` and other attributes

Type generator

The metadata feature also provides automatically generated type definitions for easy interoperability through the `NativeTypes` feature. The availability is coupled to the registration of `Feature.Metadata`. You can disable the `NativeTypes` feature with the following code:

```
using ServiceStack;
using Funq;

public override void Configure(Container container)
{
   this.Plugins.RemoveAll(arg => arg is NativeTypesFeature);
}
```

The following languages are covered by automatic generation:

- **C#** via `/types/csharp`
- **F#** via `/types/fsharp`
- **Java** via `/types/java`
- **Swift** via `/types/swift`
- **TypeScript** via `/types/typescript.d`
- **Vb.Net** via `/types/vbnet`

This is a legitimate alternative to sharing a model assembly in several projects and especially for the problems with interoperability issues of different languages, when there is no globally usable assembly to share.

Additional to the type affine generation, there's also a more generic variant available at `/types/metadata` that provides a more universal and language agnostic definition of your operations.

You can retrieve and customize the configuration of the type generator with the following code:

```
using Funq;
using ServiceStack;

public override void Configure(Container container)
{
    var nativeTypesFeature = this.GetPlugin<NativeTypesFeature>();
    var metadataTypesConfig =
    nativeTypesFeature.MetadataTypesConfig;
}
```

You can customize the configuration with the following properties:

- `BaseUrl` (default: `null`, inferred by the request's absolute path): This defines the URL that gets rendered as a comment, to reflect the origin of the documentation.
- `MakePartial` (default: `true`, only applicable for .NET): This allows the consumers of the generated types to extend the classes easily, by making the classes `partial`.
- `MakeVirtual` (default: `true`, only applicable for .NET): This customization adds the `virtual` keyword to property definitions, to allow interception of getters and setters in derived classes.

- `BaseClass` (default: `null`, only applicable for Swift): This defines a base class that should be injected in the output.

- `Package` (default: `null`, only applicable for Java): This defines a package that should be injected in the output.

- `AddReturnMarker` (default: `true`): This controls the forced adding of `IReturn<T>` even if the RequestDTO is not annotated with `IReturn<T>`, where `T` is inferred by the convention of the request's class name being suffixed with `Response`.

- `AddDescriptionAsComments` (default: `true`): Either the description attached via `Description` or `Api` attribute can be added as comments of classes.

- `AddDataContractAttributes` (default: `false`): This defines whether `DataContract` and `DataMember` attributes should be added to classes and properties.

- `AddIndexesToDataMembers` (default: `false`): If enabled, `DataMember` attributes that are rendered due to the `AddDataContractAttributes` setting include an explicit order.

- `AddGeneratedCodeAttributes` (default: `false`, only applicable for .NET): Controls the injection of `System.CodeDom.Compiler.GeneratedCodeAttribute` annotations, which render the actually used ServiceStack version.

- `AddImplicitVersion` (default: `null`): By setting this property to any integer value, a `Version` property with the provided value gets added to the output.

- `AddResponseStatus` (default: `false`): If this property is set to `true`, the `ResponseStatus` property that gets returned only if either an exception occurs or validation fails, is included explicitly.

- `AddServiceStackTypes` (default: `true`, only applicable for Typescript): If set to true, the definition of ServiceStack types, such as `IReturn<T>` and `IReturnVoid` are added to the output.

- `AddModelExtensions` (default: `true`, only applicable for Swift): Adds extensions for converting to string, JSON, and object to the output.

- `AddPropertyAccessors` (default: `true`, only applicable for Java): Adds get and set methods to the output.

- `ExcludeGenericBaseTypes` (default: `true`, only applicable for Swift): If set to `true`, the Generic Base Type does not get included in the output.

- `SettersReturnThis` (default: `true`, only applicable for Java): If set to `true`, setters return the actual instance to provide a fluent interface.

- `MakePropertiesOptional` (default: `true`, only applicable for Swift): If set to `true`, all properties are rendered as optional.

- `AddDefaultXmlNamespace` (default: `null`, only applicable for .NET): If `AddDataContractAttributes` is set to `true`, you can override the default XML namespace `http://schemas.servicestack.net/types` with a custom value.

- `MakeDataContractsExtensible` (default: `false`, only applicable for .NET): This adds a generic bucket property `ExtensionData` to the output that can be used to store data outside of the schema.

- `InitializeCollections` (default: `true`, only applicable for .NET and Swift): This controls the initialization of collection properties in the constructor, which is helpful to avoid null-checks and possible `NullReferenceExceptions`.

- `DefaultNamespaces` (default: [`System`, `System.Collections`, `System. Collections.Generic`, `System.Collections.Generic`, `ServiceStack`, `ServiceStack.DataAnnotations`], only applicable for .NET): This defines the default for `Imports`, `open`, and `using` directives.

- `DefaultImports` (default: see the definition of concrete generators, only applicable for Swift, Java, and TypeScript): The same as `DefaultNamespaces` but for other languages.

- `IncludeTypes` (default: `[]`): The whitelist for rendered types.

- `ExcludeTypes` (default: `[]`): The blacklist for rendered types.

- `GlobalNamespace` (default: `null`, applicable to all languages except Swift): This provides an override for the project's namespace in the output.

- `IgnoreTypes` (default: `null`): This is similar to `ExcludeTypes`, but a typed blacklist for rendered types.

- `ExportAttributes` (default: [`FlagsAttribute`, `ApiAttribute`, `ApiResponseAttribute`, `ApiMemberAttribute`, `StringLengthAttribute`, `DefaultAttribute`, `IgnoreAttribute`, `IngoreDataMemberAttribute`, `MetaAttribute`, `RequiredAttribute`, `ReferencesAttribute`, `StringLengthAttribute`, `AutoQueryViewerAttribute`, `AutoQueryViewerFieldAttribute`]): This provides a whitelist for attributes not associated with the serialization stack that should get rendered to the output.

- `IgnoreTypesInNamespace` (default: `[ServiceStack, ServiceStack.` `Auth, ServiceStack.Caching, ServiceStack.Configuration,` `ServiceStack.Data, ServiceStack.IO, ServiceStack.Logging,` `ServiceStack.Messaging, ServiceStack.Model,ServiceStack.Redis,` `ServiceStackWeb, ServiceStack.Admin, ServiceStack.NativeTypes,` `ServiceStack.Api.Swagger]`): This is the blacklist of namespaces whose types should not be rendered.

- `ExportTypes` (default: `[IGet, IPost, IPut, IDelete, IPatch]`): This whitelist holds all the CLR types that should be allowed to be rendered. If you add an enum type, the feature also renders the definition of the very enum.

Additionally to these global settings the concrete language generators have unified properties to define the language specific translations, such as `TypeAliases`, `KeyWords`, `ArrayTypes`, `DictionaryTypes`, and collections for proper escaping property names. Furthermore, there are some very specific settings available for the following generator classes:

- `ServiceStack.NativeTypes.Java.JavaGenerator`:
    - `DefaultGlobalNamespace` (default: `dto`): This provides the default namespace if the `GlobalNamespace` property of the configuration is not set.
    - `DefaultImports` (default: `[java.math.*, java.util.*, net.` `servicestack.client.*]`): This defines the default imports for the `DefaultImports` property of the configuration.
    - `GSonAnnotationsNamespace` (default: `com.google.gson.` `annotations.*`)
    - `GSonReflectNamespace` (default: `com.google.gson.reflect.*`)
    - `AddGsonImport` (set-only)

- `ServiceStack.NativeTypes.TypeScript.TypeScriptGenerator`:
    - `DefaultImports` (default: `[]`): This defines the default imports for the `DefaultImports` property of the configuration.

- `ServiceStack.NativeTypes.Swift.SwiftGenerator`:
    - `DefaultImports` (default: `[foundation]`): This defines the default imports for the `DefaultImports` property of the configuration.

 The output of the generator is primarily used by the IDE plugins of ServiceStack, which let you add references to a service. More information on these plugins can be found at `https://github.` `com/ServiceStack/ServiceStack/wiki/Add-ServiceStack-` `Reference`.

Querying your service with Swagger

Documenting your API is only one part of making it explorable, you can also offer a way to play with your API by generating requests and display their responses, along with the possibility to read through the documentation.

Therefore, Swagger, which is an advanced testing environment, is available for any ServiceStack service and can be enabled by adding the `ServiceStack.Api.Swagger` NuGet package to your solution. Additionally, you have to add a `SwaggerFeature` object to your host's configuration, as shown:

```
using Funq;
using ServiceStack;

public override void Configure(Container container)
{
   this.Plugins.Add(new SwaggerFeature());
}
```

This will offer a new link in the plugin section of the metadata page available at `/metadata`, as shown in the following figure:

XSDS:

- Service Types
- Wcf Data Types
- Wcf Collection Types

WSDLS:

- soap11
- soap12

Plugin Links:

- Swagger UI

Debug Info:

- Operations Metadata
- Request Info

This link points to `/swagger-ui/` in the default configuration. There, you will find the following interface, which also includes documentation on the service and its operations:

We can now populate the parameters and actually execute an operation and inspect the result, as shown in the following screenshot:

To further customize the available documentation, you can annotate your RequestDTOs with the `ApiResponse` attribute to add reasons as to why requests can fail.

```
using Sytem.Net;
using ServiceStack;

[ApiResponse(HttpStatusCode.InternalServerError, "There was an
  exception during greeting.")]
public class Hello : IReturn<HelloResponse>
{
  public string Name { get; set; }
  public Volume Volume { get; set; }
}
```

The possible response statuses are added at the bottom of the sandbox section, as shown:

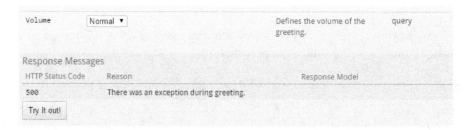

Besides the additional response status, Swagger also uses the additional properties of the `ApiMember` attribute. The most important one is the `ExcludeInSchema` attribute, which controls the documentation of the property for PUT and POST requests. In the following screenshot the `Volume` property is excluded from the payload:

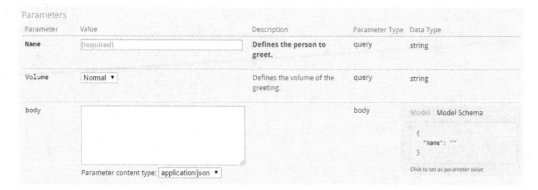

You can use the `System.Runtime.Serialization.IgnoreDataMember` attribute to fully exclude a property from being included in the Swagger interface in an opt-out scenario. In an opt-in scenario you just need to skip annotating the property with the `System.Runtime.Serialization.DataMember` attribute.

To add multiple descriptions and specifications to a property, you can limit the `ApiMember` attribute with its `Verb` and `Route` property for specific scenarios.

Further options to document are available with the `ParameterType` property that defines the storage of the value and can be one of `path`, `query`, `body`, `form`, or `header`, `DataType`, and `AllowMultiple`.

The value of `ParameterType` defines where Swagger has to add the value of the property on a request.

- `path`: The value of the member is set on the RequestDTO.
- `query`: The value is stored as a query string parameter.
- `body`: There should not be more than one property defined as the body parameter, which reflects the content of the HTTP body.
- `form`: The `Content-Type` of the request will be changed to `application/x-www-form-urlencoded` to reflect a form request, and the value is stored in the forms collection.
- `header`: The value is stored in a corresponding HTTP header. To follow best practice with custom HTTP headers, you should adapt the naming of your member to be prefixed with *X-*:

  ```
  [ApiMember(Name = "X-Name", ParameterType = "header"]
  public string Name { get; set; }
  ```

Furthermore, operations must be annotated with at least one `Route` attribute to show up in Swagger.

The `SwaggerFeature` class offers the following properties for adjustments:

- `DisableAutoDtoInBodyParam` (default: `false`): The automatically appended body parameter in the sandbox section can be turned off with this property.
- `ModelFilter`: This provides a hook to adapt a registered model.
- `ModelPropertyFilter`: This provides a hook to adapt a registered property of a model.

- UseBootstrapTheme (default: `false`): This rewrites the plugin link to `/swagger-ui-bootstrap/`, which features a bootstrap theme.

- UseCamelCaseModelPropertyNames (default: `false`): Lets you switch the casing of property names to "CamelCase", unless annotated with a `DataMember` attribute.

- UseLowercaseUnderscoreModelPropertyNames (default: `false`): This only works in combination with UseCamelCaseModelPropertyNames and further customizes the casing of property names.

- ResourceFilterPattern (default: `null`): This defines a regular expression that is used to filter operations by their type names, as only matching names are exposed.

- LogoUrl (default: `[//raw.githubusercontent.com/ServiceStack/Assets/master/img/artwork/logo-24.png]`): Lets you adapt the source of the rendered logo.

Querying your service with Postman

Another approach to offer a sandbox for your API is to feed the Postman plugin of your browser with certain metadata to offer automatic discovery of your operations.

Postman is a Google Chrome plugin that can be launched as a stand-alone application to help developers work with APIs.

The corresponding feature comes shipped with ServiceStack and just needs activation in your app host's configuration.

```
using Funq;
using ServiceStack;

public override void Configure(Container container)
{
    this.Plugins.Add(new PostmanFeature());
}
```

The generated Postman collection is now available at `/postman` and can be added to your collections.

The Postman feature offers the following properties for adaptions, just like outer features:

- AtRestPath (default: `/postman`): This lets you adapt the URL to expose the Postman collection.

- `DefaultLabelFmt` (default: `[type]`): This lets you define a format for the title of each operation in the collection, if you do not inject a certain label style with the URL, such as `?label=type` or `?label=route`). The possible fragments are `route` (for example `/hello/{Name}`), `type` (for example `Hello`) and `english` (only available on the second position; English casing of the type), which are separated by a colon.

- `DefaultVerbsForAny` (default: `GET`): The routes for `Any` methods are only exposed as verbs added to the collection.

- `EnableSessionExport` (default: Is in debug mode?): If enabled it lets you inject session information (`ssopt`, `sspid`, `ssid`) along with the collection as query string parameters.

- `FriendlyTypeNames`: This holds a dictionary to translate CLR types to Postman types, for example to translate `TimeSpan` with `string`.

- `Headers` (default: `Accept: application/json`): This lets you inject additional headers to the collection entries, which then gets sent along with a request.

Versioning requests

Evolution of API is a natural aspect, and is more desirable than a complete rewrite of your API. However, when it comes to pushing these changes to production you may encounter interoperability issues with legacy clients. One key factor when thinking about and designing the changes of your interface, is not to put the whole environment in a lock-down state until all legacy clients are updated.

One solution to this problem is the introduction of versioning to your DTOs. Consider the following request DTO:

```
// Version 0
public class Hello
{
    public string Name { get; set; }
}
```

After some time, you realize that it would be better to split the name into forename and surname, so you adapt the `Hello` class as:

```
// Version 1
public class Hello
{
    public string Forename { get; set; }
    public string Surname { get; set; }
}
```

If you try to call your operation with an instance of `Hello` from `version` `0`, the call will result in a broken result (`Forename` and `Surname` get initialized with `null`, making the output useless).

To overcome this issue, we'll make `Hello` version affine:

```
// Version 1
using ServiceStack;

public class Hello : IHasVersion
{
  public int Version { get; set; }
  public string Name { get; set; }
  public string Forename { get; set; }
  public string Surname { get; set; }
}
```

As you can see, `Hello` is now implementing `IHasVersion`, which declares a `Version` property, and still contains the legacy `Name` property. So, now we can adapt our logic of the service implementation, based on the value of the `Version` property.

```
using ServiceStack;

public class Service : IService,
                       IAnyVoid<Hello>
{
  public void Any(Hello request)
  {
    if (request.Version == 0)
    {
      // {
      //   Name = "John Doe",
      //   Forename = null,
      //   Surname = null
      // }
    }
    else if (request.Version == 1)
    {
      // {
      //   Name = null,
      //   Forename = "John",
      //   Surname = "Doe"
      // }
    }
  }
}
```

This approach gives you an explicit access to versions, as code based on a concrete version is naturally grouped together. This makes the task of dropping support for legacy versions a lookup of the appropriate group.

As mentioned earlier in this chapter, you can add an implicit version to the type generator. This should be used upfront to ensure the inclusion of versions for clients, generated with by ServiceStack plugin, right from the start.

To add an implicit version after the initial deploy, you can adapt the model factory of the JSON configuration that is used to deserialize requests into objects, as shown:

```
using ServiceStack;
using ServiceStack.Text;

JsConfig.ModelFactory = type => () =>
{
  var instance = type.CreateInstance();
  var iHasVersion = instance as IHasVersion;
  if (iHasVersion != null)
  {
    iHasVersion.Version = 0;
  }
  return instance;
};
```

To make use of the automatic population of the Version property with JsonServiceClient instances, you can simply use its Version property which automatically initializes the version to all DTOs that implement IHasVersion:

```
using ServiceStack;

using (var jsonServiceClient = new JsonServiceClient(url)
                               {
                                 Version = 1
                               })
{
  // perform operations
}
```

As an alternative you can also suffix the URL with for example ?v=1 to inject a version

Another approach to add versioning later on, is to add an extension bag for SOAP endpoints to store values that are out of the scheme:

```
using System.Runtime.Serialization;

public class Hello : IExtensibleDataObject
{
  public string Name { get; set; }
  public ExtensionDataObject ExtensionData { get; set; }
}
```

As mentioned earlier in this chapter, as with the Version property, you can make the generated classes in the type generator implement the IExtensibleDataObject interface by setting the MakeDataContractsExtensible property of your type generator's configuration to true.

The most important part of versioning is a defensive evolution of your contract, by keeping in mind legacy clients. This is relevant even though the built-in serializers of JSON and JSV support adaptations of your properties to a certain degree. The following adaptations do not cause any issue:

- Changing int to long
- List<T> to HashSet<T>
- Changing the type of a property T to T?
- Changing the type of a complex property to Dictionary<string, object>

Additionally, it is advisable to use a custom global XML namespace with SOAP endpoints, by adapting your configuration to:

```
using Funq;
using ServiceStack;

public override void Configure(Container container)
{
  this.SetConfig(new HostConfig
  {
    WsdlServiceNamespace = "http://schemas.foobar.org/types"
  });
}
```

Validating your requests

Supplementary to documentation, when implementing an API there should also be a validation included, as the most important mantra is: don't trust user input.

Whatever validation you will implement in your service, you should start off by implement the IHasResponseStatus interface on your response DTO:

```
using ServiceStack;

public class HelloResponse : IHasResponseStatus
{
  public string Result { get; set; }
  public ResponseStatus ResponseStatus { get; set; }
}
```

This will guarantee that any exception will get serialized into the ResponseStatus property. Additionally, the following exceptions will adapt the HTTP status code of the request:

- ArgumentException and descendants returns 400 BadRequest
- NotImplementedException returns 405 MethodNotAllowed
- Any other exception returns 500 InternalServerError

You can add custom mappings by adding a translation to the MapExceptionToStatusCode property of your host's config, which also supports inheritance:

```
using System;
using System.Collections.Generic;
using System.Net;
using Funq;
using ServiceStack;

public override void Configure(Container container)
{
  this.SetConfig(new HostConfig
  {
    MapExceptionToStatusCode = new Dictionary<Type, int>
    {
      { typeof (FooException), (int) HttpStatusCode.ServiceUnavailable
      } // will also be returned for descendants of FooException
    }
  });
}
```

As an alternative, you can also implement the `IHasStatusCode` interface in your custom exception class, to reflect the HTTP status code:

```
using System;
using System.Net;
using ServiceStack.Model;

public class FooException : Exception,
                                        IHasStatusCode
{
    // ctor left out on porpuse here

    public int StatusCode
    {
      get
      {
        return (int) HttpStatusCode.ServiceUnavailable;
      }
    }
}
```

Moreover to the automatic mapping of HTTP status codes you can also use the `ServiceStack.HttpError` class to create exceptions, by either instantiating a customized one with a `System.Net.HttpStatusCode` value or using any of the static methods `NotFound(message)`, `Conflict(message)`, `Forbidden(message)`, or `Unauthorized(message)`.

 The inclusion of the stack trace is available in the debug mode only.

Using a `JsonServiceClient` instance to interact with your service will throw a `ServiceStack.WebServiceException` object that can be used to obtain more information on the exception of the error, regardless of the implementation of `IHasResponseStatus`.

Adding value checking to your code manually can get quite cumbersome and fragmented. Therefore ServiceStack offers `the` validation feature, which you can enable in your host's configuration.

```
using Funq;
using ServiceStack;
using ServiceStack.Validation;

public override void Configure(Container container)
{
  this.Plugins.Add(new ValidationFeature());
}
```

The validation rules are offloaded into separate classes, which can be added either by auto-discovering or explicit injection.

```
public override void Configure(Container container)
{
  this.Plugins.Add(new ValidationFeature());
  container.RegisterValidators(typeof (HelloService).Assembly);
  container.RegisterValidators(ReusceScope.Container,
                               typeof (HelloService).Assembly);
  container.RegisterValidator(typeof (FooValidator);
  container.RegisterValidator(typeof (FooValidator),
                              ReuseScope.Container);
}
```

 The validation is realized through the `FluentValidation` project (`https://github.com/JeremySkinner/FluentValidation`) by Jeremy Skinner that also contains a superb documentation on all the available validation rules (`https://github.com/JeremySkinner/FluentValidation/wiki/c.-Built-In-Validators`).

 The validation is put into effect through request filters of requests and messages, which is implemented in the `ServiceStack.Validation.ValidationFilters.RequestFilter` method.

A demo validator for our `Hello` DTO will look like this:

```
using ServiceStack.FluentValidation;

public class HelloValidator : AbstractValidator<Hello>
{
```

```
    public HelloValidator()
    {
      this.RuleFor(arg => arg.Name)
          .NotEmpty();
    }
}
```

You can further customize the rule with the following extension methods:

```
this.RuleFor(arg => arg.Name)
    .NotEmpty()
    .WithMessage("This is a static message");

this.RuleFor(arg => arg.Name)
    .NotEmpty()
    .WithLocalizedMessage(() => Resources.LocalizedMessage);

this.RuleFor(arg => arg.Name)
    .NotEmpty()
    .WithErrorCode("MyCustomCode");

this.RuleFor(arg => arg.Name)
    .NotEmpty()
    .WithName("FooName");

this.RuleFor(arg => arg.Name)
    .NotEmpty()
    .WithState(dto => new CustomState());
```

You can also scope the rules to a HTTP verb, by simply using the `RuleSet` method:

```
public class HelloValidator : AbstractValidator<Hello>
{
  public HelloValidator()
  {
    this.RuleFor(arg => arg.Name)
        .NotEmpty();

    this.RuleSet(ApplyTo.Post, () =>
    {
      this.RuleFor(arg => arg.Volume)
          .NotEqual(Volume.Loud);
    });
  }
}
```

ServiceStack triggers rules that are not assigned to an HTTP verb and the rules for the concrete HTTP verb, according to the incoming request.

As an alternative to these pre-built rules, there's also the possibility to create a completely customized validator.

```
using ServiceStack.FluentValidation.Validators;

public class MaxLengthValidator : PropertyValidator
{
  public MaxLengthValidator(int maxLength)
   : base ("{PropertyName} is longer than {MaxLength}",
          "MaxLength")
  {
    this.MaxLength = maxLength;
  }

  public int MaxLength { get; set; }

  protected override bool IsValid(PropertyValidatorContext
  context)
  {
    var propertyValue = context.PropertyValue as string;
    if (string.IsNullOrEmpty(propertyValue))
    {
      return true;
    }

    var maxLength = this.MaxLength;
    var success = propertyValue.Length < maxLength;
    if (!success)
    {
      context.MessageFormatter.AppendArgument("MaxLength",
                                             maxLength);
    }
    return success;
  }
}
```

This validator tries to convert the provided value to a string and validate its length against the set `MaxLength`. To make use of this validator, you need to assign it in a validation rule, as shown:

```
this.RuleFor(arg => arg.Name)
    .SetValidator(new MaxLengthValidator(10));
```

 This custom `MaxLengthValidator` is just an example and the built-in `LengthValidator` should be used instead!

Even though ServiceStack applies the validation rules automatically to each matching request, you can also trigger the validation manually with the `Validate` method or `ValidateAndThrow` extension method.

To follow the Inversion of Control pattern you can define a validator property in your service class that gets initialized and auto-wired as soon as the service gets resolved:

```
using ServiceStack;
using ServiceStack.FluentValidation;

public class FooService: Service,
                         IAny<Hello>
{
  public IValidator<Hello> HelloValidator { get; set; }

  public object Any(Hello request)
  {
    var validationResult = this.HelloValidator.Validate(request);
    this.HelloValidator.ValidateAndThrow(request);
    // actual implementation
  }
}
```

Querying the registered ValdationRules with an API

Adding validation rules to your code-base also calls for a certain kind of documentation. You can either gather, push, and adapt the information on every change or offer an operation that prints all the currently applied validation rules for a type.

This information can be made available through the following response DTO:

```
using System.Collections.Generic;
using ServiceStack;

public class ValidationRuleSetResponse : IHasResponseStatus
{
  public List<ValidationRulesOfProperty> Rules { get; set; }
  public ResponseStatus ResponseStatus { get; set; }
}
```

The `ValidationRulesSetResponse` class contains a set of `ValidationRulesOfProperty` objects, which are defined as follows:

```
using System.Collections.Generic;

public class ValidationRulesOfProperty
{
  public string PropertyName { get; set; }
  public List<string> ValidationRules { get; set; }
}
```

The response is simply returned to the following RequestDTO and handler:

```
using ServiceStack;

[Route("/validationRules/{TypeName}")]
public class ValidationRuleSet : IReturn<ValidationRuleSetResponse>
{
  public string TypeName { get; set; }
}

public class ValidationService : Service,
                                 IGet<ValidationRuleSet>
{
  public object Get(ValidationRuleSet request)
  {
    // TODO logic
  }
}
```

This operation is reached by calling, for example `/validationRules/Hello`, and it returns multiple validation rules to each property of the model.

To get the validation rules of a model we need to find the validator first, which is done with the following code:

```
using System.Linq;
using ServiceStack;

public object Get(ValidationRuleSet request)
{
    var typeName = request.TypeName;
    var assembly = typeof (HelloService).Assembly;
    var type = assembly.GetExportedTypes()
                        .FirstOrDefault(arg => arg.Name == typeName);
    if (type == null)
    {
        throw HttpError.NotFound("Type {0} cannot be
        found".Fmt(typeName));
    }
    var validatorType = typeof (IValidator<>).MakeGenericType(type);
    var methodInfo = typeof (Service).GetMethod("TryResolve");
    var validator = (IValidator)
    methodInfo.MakeGenericMethod(validatorType)
                        .Invoke(this, null);
    if (validator == null)
    {
        throw HttpError.NotFound("Validator for type {0} cannot be
        found".Fmt(typeName));
    }

    return this.GetValidationRuleSetResponse(type, validator);
}
```

This code is considered a violation of the IoC pattern as the operation resolves a dependency on its own instead of letting the container pass an instance. However, we need to take this path as the underlying type is passed to the operation dynamically.

The actual logic of gathering the validation rules gives a deep insight into the
internals of `FluentValidation`:

```
using System;
using System.Linq;
using ServiceStack.FluentValidation;

public object GetValidationRuleSetResponse(Type type,
                                           IValidator validator)
{
  var instance = type.CreateInstance();
  var validationContext = new ValidationContext(instance);
  var validationDescriptor = validator.CreateDescriptor();
  var rules = validationDescriptor.GetMembersWithValidators()
                        .Select(arg =>
  {
    var propertyName = arg.Key;
    return this.GetValidationRulesOfProperty(propertyName,
                                             validatorDescriptor,
                                             validationContext);
  })
                        .ToList();
  var validationRuleSetResponse = new ValidationRuleSetResponse
  {
    Rules = rules
  };
  return validationRuleSetResponse;
})
```

This code creates a new instance of the DTO type. The instance is then used
to create a `ValidationContext` object, which is used to render the message.
The context is finally used to create a `ValidatorDescriptor` object, which is
used to retrieve all available rules.

The next step is to gather all the rules of one property:

```
using System.Linq;
using ServiceStack.FluentValidation;
using ServiceStack.FluentValidation.Internal;

public ValidationRulesOfProperty
                    GetValidationRulesOfProperty(string
                    propertyName,
```

```
                                IValidatorDescriptor
                                validatorDescriptor,
                                ValidationContext validationContext)
{
   var validationRules =
   validatorDescriptor.GetRulesForMember(propertyName)
                       .OfType<PropertyRule>()
                       .SelectMany(rule =>
   {
      return this.GetValidationRules(validationContext,
                                     rule,
                                     propertyName);
   })
                       .ToList();
   var validationRulesOfProperty = new ValidationRulesOfProperty
   {
      PropertyName = propertyName,
      ValidationRules = validationRules
   };
   return validationRulesOfProperty;
}
```

By calling the `GetRulesForMember` method, we retrieve a collection of `ServiceStack.FluentValidation.IValidationRule` objects that we limit to `PropertyRule` objects.

The next method mimics the implementation of the fluent validation's `ValidationRule.Validate` method. Without knowing the concrete value to validate, we need to build up the error message on our own.

```
using ServiceStack.FluentValidation;
using ServiceStack.FluentValidation.Internal;
using ServiceStack.FluentValidation.Validators;

private IEnumerable<string> GetValidationRules(ValidationContext
                                               validationContext,
                                               PropertyRule rule,
                                               string
                                               propertyName)
{
   var propertyContext = new
                         PropertyValidatorContext
                         (validationContext,
                         rule,
```

```
                              propertyName);
    propertyContext.MessageFormatter.AppendPropertyName(propertyName);

    var validationRules = rule.Validators.Select(validator =>
    {
      var messageFormatter = propertyContext.MessageFormatter;

      var comparisonValidator = validator as IComparisonValidator;
      if (comparisonValidator != null)
      {
        messageFormatter.AppendArgument("PropertyValue",
                                  comparisonValidator.
                                  ValueToCompare);
      }

      // TODO add more arguments

      var errorMessageSource = validator.ErrorMessageSource;
      var messageTemplate = errorMessageSource.GetString();
      var message = messageFormatter.BuildMessage(messageTemplate);

      return message;
    });

    return validationRules;
  }
```

This method looks a bit tough upfront, but it unwinds the beauty of FluentValidation's architecture. First off, we need to create a PropertyValidatorContext object, which is used to format the message template from a validator. The message template is retrieved from the ErrorMessageSource class' GetString method. Finally, we let the MessageFormatter object build up the message.

The only issue here is that the tuples of placeholders and their values are statically implemented in the validation framework's source. Therefore, we need to manually apply all placeholders to the formatter, which may result in a certain research on available placeholders.

This approach should just be a starting point for the publication of the applied validation rules, yet it gives a perfect insight into the validation process itself.

Summary

In this chapter the annotation based approach of adding documentation to a service was introduced, followed by the possibilities to customize the output of this documentation. Next, the Swagger and Postman features were introduced to provide a sandbox for testing your service, followed by the built-in capability to map natural evolution of an API with versioning. Finally, the validation framework of ServiceStack was introduced and finished off with querying this framework to publish the validation rules.

In the next chapter, we will look into ways of extending ServiceStack, how to write a plugin, and other points for extensions.

6
Extending ServiceStack

While implementing services, especially when you've built several components based on ServiceStack, you often find yourself in a situation where you are searching for a way to share and centralize resources or business logic, for example to streamline maintenance or looking for ways to provide extensions for ServiceStack to the community.

Thanks to the modular basis of ServiceStack, which is used throughout the core of ServiceStack itself, you can develop plugins to provide functionalities for others.

In this chapter we will cover the following topics:

- Writing your own plugin
- Intercepting request and response
- Registering new services and endpoints from within plugins

Writing your own plugin

ServiceStack allows you to write your own plugin by implementing the `IPlugin` interface that resides in the root namespace (`ServiceStack`). It needs to be added to the `Plugins` collection of your host upon configuration.

```
using Funq;
using ServiceStack;

public class AppHost : AppSelfHostBase
{
  public override void Configure(Container container)
  {
    this.Plugins.Add(new FooPlugin());
  }
```

```
  }

  public class FooPlugin : IPlugin
  {
    public void Register(IAppHost appHost)
    {
    }
  }
```

The difference between `this.Plugins.Add` and `this.LoadPlugin` is very small and is as follows:

- `this.Plugins.Add` adds an instance to the registration queue that gets iterated through after host initialization.

- `this.LoadPlugin` safely registers the provided `IPlugin` instance. If the host is already initialized, it executes the registration routine, and otherwise calls `this.Plugins.Add` to add the instance to the queue.

You can extend your plugin further by implementing the `IPreInitPlugin` interface and/or the `IPostInitPlugin` interface, which gives you access to certain states of the application host.

```
using ServiceStack;

public class FooPlugin : IPlugin,
                         IPreInitPlugin,
                         IPostInitPlugin
{
  public void Configure(IAppHost appHost)
  {
    // IPreInitPlugin
  }

  public void Register(IAppHost appHost)
  {
    // IPlugin
  }

  public void AfterPluginsLoaded(IAppHost appHost)
  {
    // IPostInitPlugin
  }
}
```

As a result of passing an `IAppHost` instance to the methods, you have full access to the host, its configuration, filters, services, and so on.

Intercepting requests and responses

A very basic scenario that is perfectly applicable amongst multiple services in a distributed environment is the need for a global identifier that travels from top to bottom of every request. This is often needed to determine which request to one API caused which request to another API; for example, to trace all the operations caused by a certain button-click in the UI.

This can be achieved by generating an identifier in the first service call and storing it along with the request. Whenever a service boundary is crossed, for example by forwarding the request to another service, the current identifier needs to be injected into that call.

First, we will define an interface that can be implemented by requests and responses to pass the identifier outside the scope of HTTP boundaries (in essence for MQ scenarios):

```
public interface IHasRequestIdentifier
{
   string RequestIdentifier { get; set; }
}
```

Additionally to this storage, we will also attach the identifier to the request's Items property for HTTP scenarios. The basic skeleton holds the key to store the identifier along with the request and response and also contains the GenerateRequestIdentifier method to generate a new identifier when none is supplied:

```
using System;
using ServiceStack;

public partial class RequestIdentifierPlugin
{
   public const string RequestIdentifierKey =
   "X-RequestIdentifier";

   public string GenerateRequestIdentifier()
   {
      return Guid.NewGuid()
               .ToString("N");
   }
}
```

First, we will extend this skeleton to read an identifier provided by a request and store it for further access, as follows:

```csharp
using System;
using ServiceStack;
using ServiceStack.Web;

public partial class RequestIdentifierPlugin : IPlugin
{

  public override void Register(IAppHost appHost)
  {
    appHost.GlobalRequestFilters.Add(this.InterceptRequest);
  }

  private void InterceptRequest(IRequest request,
                                IResponse response,
                                object dto)
  {
    var requestIdentifier = request.GetRequestIdentifier();
    if (string.IsNullOrEmpty(requestIdentifier))
    {
      var hasRequestIdentifier = dto as IHasRequestIdentifier;
      if (hasRequestIdentifier == null)
      {
        requestIdentifier = this.GenerateRequestIdentifier();
      }
      else
      {
        requestIdentifier = hasRequestIdentifier.RequestIdentifier;
        if (string.IsNullOrEmpty(requestIdentifier))
        {
          requestIdentifier = this.GenerateRequestIdentifier();
          hasRequestIdentifier.RequestIdentifier = requestIdentifier;
        }
      }
```

```
        request.SetItem(RequestIdentifierKey,
                        requestIdentifier);
    }
    else
    {
      var hasRequestIdentifier = dto as IHasRequestIdentifier;
      if (hasRequestIdentifier != null)
      {
        hasRequestIdentifier.RequestIdentifier = requestIdentifier;
      }
    }
  }
}

public static class RequestIdentifierExtensions
{
  public static string GetRequestIdentifier(this IRequest request)
  {
    return request.GetItemStringValue(RequestIdentifierKey) ??
    request.GetParamInRequestHeader(RequestIdentifierKey)
  }
}
```

The logic is based on the following sequence:

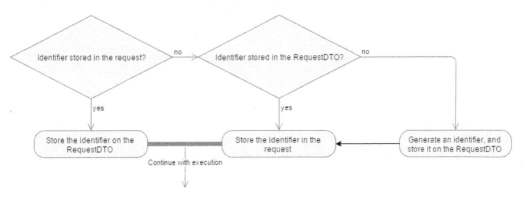

When intercepting a request, the code first tries to get an identifier from the request's items, headers, query string, or form-data (if applicable) through the `RequestIdentifierExtensions.GetRequestIdentifier` method, which uses the `ServiceStack.RequestExtensions.GetItemStringValue` and `ServiceStack.RequestExtensions.GetParamInRequestHeader` method internally.

If no identifier is found, the code tries to read the identifier from the DTO (if applicable), or otherwise generates one and applies it to the DTO (if applicable). If an identifier is found, it gets added to the DTO (if applicable).

This serves the following two scenarios:

- A request that implements the `IHasRequestIdentifier` interface can inject an identifier into the execution pipe by setting the `RequestIdentifier` property of the request.
- A request can inject an identifier through a query string, HTTP headers, or form-data, where the key is `X-RequestIdentifier`. Furthermore to request interception, the plugin also tries to attach the identifier to the returned DTO, as well as the HTTP headers:

```
public partial class RequestIdentifierPlugin : IPlugin
{
  public void Register(IAppHost appHost)
  {
    appHost.GlobalRequestFilters.Add (this.InterceptRequest);
    appHost.GlobalResponseFilters.Add(this.InterceptResponse);
  }

  private void InterceptResponse(IRequest request,
                                 IResponse response,
                                 object dto)
  {
    var requestIdentifier = request.GetRequestIdentifier();

    var hasRequestIdentifier = dto as IHasRequestIdentifier;
    if (hasRequestIdentifier != null)
    {
      hasRequestIdentifier.RequestIdentifier =
      requestIdentifier;
    }

    response.AddHeader(RequestIdentifierKey,
                       requestIdentifier);
  }
}
```

Finally, a global method to retrieve the identifier of the current request is
introduced to the code; this can be used to access the identifier in, for example
logging scenarios:

```
public partial class RequestIdentifierPlugin
{
  public static string GetRequestIdentifier(IRequest request = null)
  {
    if (request == null)
    {
      request = HostContext.GetCurrentRequest();
    }

    return request.GetRequestIdentifier()
  }
}
```

The only drawback of this approach is the need to attach the identifier manually
when crossing borders. This is due to the limited automatic assignment of request
properties, which only covers the session and versioning and is implemented in
`ServiceStack.ServiceClientBase.PopulateRequestMetadata` and called in the
private `PrepareWebRequest` method.

To overcome this limitation, you can extend your targeted service client class
(for example `ServiceStack.JsonServiceClient`) and add such assignments
yourself after reading the identifier with `RequestIdentifierPlugin.
GetRequestIdentifier`.

```
using System.IO;
using ServiceStack;
using ServiceStack.Web;

public class RequestIdentifierJsonServiceClient :
  JsonServiceClient, IHasRequestIdentifier
{
  public string RequestIdentifier { get; set; }

  public RequestIdentifierJsonServiceClient()
  {
  }
```

```
public RequestIdentifierJsonServiceClient(string baseUri)
  : base (baseUri)
{
}


public RequestIdentifierJsonServiceClient(string
syncReplyBaseUri, string asyncOneWayBaseUri)
  : base(syncReplyBaseUri,
         asyncOneWayBaseUri)
{
}


public override void SerializeToStream(IRequest requestContext,
                                       object request,
                                       Stream stream)
{
  var hasRequestIdentifier = request as IHasRequestIdentifier;
  if (hasRequestIdentifier != null)
  {
    hasRequestIdentifier.RequestIdentifier =
    this.RequestIdentifier;
  }
  base.SerializeToStream(requestContext,
                         request,
                         stream);
}
}
```

The newly introduced RequestIdentifierJsonServiceClient is capable of populating any request of type IHasRequestIdentifier with the injected request identifier:

```
public class Service: IService,
                      IAny<FooRequest>
{
  public object Any(FooRequest request)
  {
  var forwardedRequest = /* create your DTO */;
    var requestIdentifier =
    RequestIdentifierPlugin.GetRequestIdentifier();
    using (var jsonServiceClient = new
    RequestIdentifierJsonServiceClient(url)
          {
             RequestIdentifier = requestIdentifier
          })
```

```
    {
      jsonServiceClient.Post(forwardedRequest);
    }
  }
}
```

Additionally, we can introduce the following extension method to introduce a factory for requests, which get published to a MQ:

```
using ServiceStack;
public static T Create<T>(this Service service) where T :
IHasRequestIdentifier, new()
{
  var requestIdentifier = service.Request.GetRequestIdentifier();
  var instance = new T
  {
    RequestIdentifier = requestIdentifier
  };
  return instance;
}
```

This extension method can be used in your service, as shown:

```
public object Any(FooRequest request)
{
  var hello = this.Create<Hello>();
  this.MessageProducer.Publish(hello);
}
```

Registering new services and endpoints

Apart from the registration of filters, you can also add services to any application host by simply calling `RegisterService` on the provided host object.

To show you a real life scenario, we will implement a plugin that restricts the throughput of your services. This plugin will also register a service that we can use to inspect the current throughput of the service.

We will start off with the creation of an attribute to define the maximum throughput of an operation.

```
using System;
using ServiceStack;
```

```
public class ThrottleRestrictionAttribute : Attribute
{
  public const string MinuteAbbreviation = "m";
  public const string HourAbbreviation = "h";
  public const string DayAbbreviation = "d";

  public int PerMinute { get; set; }
  public int PerHour { get; set; }
  public int PerDay { get; set; }

  public int GetMaximum(string durationAbbreviation)
  {
    switch (durationAbbreviation)
    {
      case MinuteAbbreviation:
        return this.PerMinute;
      case HourAbbreviation:
        return this.PerHour;
      case DayAbbreviation:
        return this.PerDay;
      default:
        var message = "Abbreviation {0} is
        unknown".Fmt(durationAbbreviation);
        throw new
        ArgumentOutOfRangeException(durationAbbreviation,
                        message);
    }
  }
}
```

The `ThrottleRestriction` attribute is now applied to our `Hello` request, as shown:

```
[Route("/hello/{Name}")]
[ThrottleRestriction(PerMinute = 10)]
public class Hello
{
  public string Name { get; set; }
}
```

Now, we need to implement a logic that scans through the registered operations of a host to read all the restrictions:

```
using System;
using System.Collections.Generic;
using System.Reflection;
```

```
using ServiceStack;
using ServiceStack.Web;

public partial class ThrottlePlugin : IPlugin
{
  private readonly Dictionary<Type, ThrottleRestrictionAttribute>
  _throttleRestrictionAttributes = new Dictionary<Type,
  ThrottleRestrictionAttribute>();

  public void Register(IAppHost appHost)
  {
    this.RegisterThrottleRestrictionAttributes();
  }

  private void RegisterThrottleRestrictionAttributes()
  {
    // We are iterating over all operations here and
    // reading the limits from annotated operations.
    foreach (var operation in appHost.Metadata.Operations)
    {
      var requestType = operation.RequestType;
      var throttleRestrictionAttribute =
      requestType.GetCustomAttribute
      <ThrottleRestrictionAttribute>();
      if (throttleRestrictionAttribute != null)
      {
        this._throttleRestrictionAttributes[requestType] =
        throttleRestrictionAttribute;
      }
    }
  }
}
```

Now we need to ensure that the defined restrictions are met, as shown:

```
using System;
using System.Reflection;
using ServiceStack;
using ServiceStack.Web;

public partial class ThrottlePlugin
{
  public const string CacheKeyPrefix = "__throttleCounter";
```

```
public void Register(IAppHost appHost)
{
  this.RegisterThrottleRestrictionAttributes();
  appHost.GlobalRequestFilters.Add
  (this.RejectRequestIfThrottelingApplies);
}

private void RejectRequestIfThrottelingApplies(IRequest request,
                                               IResponse response,
                                               object dto)
{
  if (dto == null)
  {
    return;
  }

  var type = dto.GetType();

  ThrottleRestrictionAttribute throttleRestrictionAttribute;
  if (!this._throttleRestrictionAttributes.TryGetValue(type,
                       out throttleRestrictionAttribute))
  {
    return;
  }

  var durationScopes = new[]
  {
    new
    {
      DurationAbbreviation =
      ThrottleRestrictionAttribute.MinuteAbbreviation,
      Duration = TimeSpan.FromMinutes(1d)
    },
    new
    {
      DurationAbbreviation =
      ThrottleRestrictionAttribute.HourAbbreviation,
      Duration = TimeSpan.FromHours(1d)
    },
    new
    {
```

```
    DurationAbbreviation =
    ThrottleRestrictionAttribute.DayAbbreviation,
    Duration = TimeSpan.FromDays(1d)
  }
};

var cacheClient = request.GetCacheClient();

var shouldThrottle = false;
foreach (var durationScope in durationScopes)
{
  var maximum =
  throttleRestrictionAttribute.GetMaximum
  (durationScope.DurationAbbreviation);
  if (maximum <= 0)
  {
    continue;
  }

  var key = "{0}|{1}|{2}|{3}".Fmt(CacheKeyPrefix,
                                  request.RemoteIp,
                                  request.OperationName,
                                  durationScope.
                                  DurationAbbreviation);

  var counter = cacheClient.Get<int>(key);

  TimeSpan expiresIn;
  if (counter > 0)
  {
    expiresIn = cacheClient.GetTimeToLive(key) ??
    durationScope.Duration;
  }
  else
  {
    expiresIn = durationScope.Duration;
  }

  cacheClient.Set(key,
                  ++counter,
                  expiresIn);
```

```
      shouldThrottle |= counter > maximum;
    }

    if (shouldThrottle)
    {
      response.StatusCode = 429; // too many requests
      response.StatusDescription = "Too many requests.";
      response.End();
    }
  }
}
```

This very basic and naive algorithm cycles through all the possible time units, increments the counter by one, and stores it back with either the original or a new expiration time.

If throttling is applied, the request is rejected with the HTTP status 429 Too Many Requests.

> If you want to implement this in an atomic way, you can take the Redis and Lua way, described by Cory Taylor at http://www.corytaylor. ca/api-throttling-with-servicestack/.

The final service that offers an inspection of these counters needs a request and response class as well as a representation of the counters:

```
using ServiceStack;

[Route("/throttlecounters")]
public sealed class ThrottleCountersRequest :
  IReturn<ThrottleCountersResponse>
{
}

public sealed class ThrottleCountersResponse
{
  public ThrottleCounter[] ThrottleCounters { get; set; }
}

public sealed class ThrottleCounter
{
```

```
    public string RemoteIp { get; set; }
    public string Operation { get; set; }
    public string DurationAbbreviation { get; set; }
    public int Counter { get; set; }
    public string ExpiresIn { get; set; }
}
```

This is the main prerequisite to implement the following service:

```
using System;
using System.Linq;
using ServiceStack;

public sealed class ThrottleService : Service,
                                      IGet<ThrottleCountersRequest>
{
  public object Get(ThrottleCountersRequest request)
  {
    var cacheKeys = this.CacheClient.GetKeysStartingWith(ThrottlePlug
in.CacheKeyPrefix)

    var counters = cacheKeys.Select(cacheKey => new
    {
      CacheKey = cacheKey,
      Counter = this.Cache.Get<int>(cacheKey),
      ExpiresIn = this.Cache.GetTimeToLive(cacheKey) ??
      TimeSpan.Zero
    });

    var throttleCountersResponse = new ThrottleCountersResponse
    {
      ThrottleCounters = counters.Select(counter =>
      {
        var throttleCounter =
        ThrottlePlugin.CreateThrottleCounter(counter.CacheKey);
        throttleCounter.Counter = counter.Counter;
        throttleCounter.ExpiresIn = counter.ExpiresIn.ToString();

        return throttleCounter;
      }).ToArray()
    };

    return throttleCountersResponse;
  }
}
```

This code iterates over all the keys that start with `__throttleCounter` and requests their value and time-to-live. This information is returned to the client with `ThrottleCounter` objects which are created in the `ThrottlePlugin`, as shown:

```
using System.Linq;
using ServiceStack;

public partial class ThrottlePlugin
{
    internal static ThrottleCounter CreateThrottleCounter(string
cacheKey)
    {
        var cacheKeyParts = cacheKey.Split('|');
        var prefix = cacheKeyParts.ElementAt(0);
        var remoteIp = cacheKeyParts.ElementAt(1);
        var operation = cacheKeyParts.ElementAt(2);
        var durationAbbreviation = cacheKeyParts.ElementAt(3);

        var throttleCounter = new ThrottleCounter
        {
            DurationAbbreviation = durationAbbreviation,
            Operation = operation,
            RemoteIp = remoteIp
        };

        return throttleCounter;
    }
}
```

Finally, the `ThrottleService` is registered:

```
using ServiceStack;

public partial class ThrottlePlugin : IPlugin
{
    public void Register(IAppHost appHost)
    {
        this.RegisterThrottleRestrictionAttributes(appHost);

        appHost.GlobalRequestFilters.Add
        (RejectRequestIfThrottelingApplies);
        appHost.RegisterService<ThrottleService>();
    }
}
```

You can now request the URL /throttlecounters to inspect all the currently available counters, as shown in the following screenshot:

```
←  →  C    localhost:5555/throttlecounters?format=json

{
    "ThrottleCounters": [
        {
            "RemoteIp": "::1",
            "Operation": "Hello",
            "DurationAbbreviation": "m",
            "Counter": 1,
            "ExpiresIn": "00:00:56.3599792"
        }
    ]
}
```

Summary

In this chapter we covered the possibilities that ServiceStack offers us to extend the core functionality by extracting globally used logic and components to plugins. First, we discussed the creation along with examples of how to manipulate the host at certain phases, then the possibility of intercepting requests and responses with and finally we finished with a practical example of how to add services inside a plugin.

Index

U

user entity
  customizing 51

V

Visual Studio Development Server 89

W

website
  requests, tracking of 112-115
**Windows Communication Framework
    (WCF) 2, 3**

Thank you for buying
Mastering ServiceStack

About Packt Publishing

Packt, pronounced 'packed', published its first book, *Mastering phpMyAdmin for Effective MySQL Management*, in April 2004, and subsequently continued to specialize in publishing highly focused books on specific technologies and solutions.

Our books and publications share the experiences of your fellow IT professionals in adapting and customizing today's systems, applications, and frameworks. Our solution-based books give you the knowledge and power to customize the software and technologies you're using to get the job done. Packt books are more specific and less general than the IT books you have seen in the past. Our unique business model allows us to bring you more focused information, giving you more of what you need to know, and less of what you don't.

Packt is a modern yet unique publishing company that focuses on producing quality, cutting-edge books for communities of developers, administrators, and newbies alike. For more information, please visit our website at www.packtpub.com.

About Packt Open Source

In 2010, Packt launched two new brands, Packt Open Source and Packt Enterprise, in order to continue its focus on specialization. This book is part of the Packt Open Source brand, home to books published on software built around open source licenses, and offering information to anybody from advanced developers to budding web designers. The Open Source brand also runs Packt's Open Source Royalty Scheme, by which Packt gives a royalty to each open source project about whose software a book is sold.

Writing for Packt

We welcome all inquiries from people who are interested in authoring. Book proposals should be sent to author@packtpub.com. If your book idea is still at an early stage and you would like to discuss it first before writing a formal book proposal, then please contact us; one of our commissioning editors will get in touch with you.

We're not just looking for published authors; if you have strong technical skills but no writing experience, our experienced editors can help you develop a writing career, or simply get some additional reward for your expertise.

ServiceStack 4 Cookbook

ISBN: 978-1-78398-656-9   Paperback: 444 pages

Over 70 recipes to create web services, build message-based apps, and work with object-relational mapping

1. Create fast, testable, maintainable web APIs using the fully-featured framework in .NET.

2. Integrate ServiceStack to add speed and simplicity to your web applications.

3. Step-by-step recipes that focus on solving real-world problems using ServiceStack.

Learning Concurrent Programming in Scala

ISBN: 978-1-78328-141-1   Paperback: 366 pages

Learn the art of building intricate, modern, scalable concurrent applications using Scala

1. Design and implement scalable and easy-to-understand concurrent applications.

2. Make the most of Scala by understanding its philosophy and harnessing the power of multicores.

3. Get acquainted with cutting-edge technologies in the field of concurrency, with a particular emphasis on practical, real-world applications.

Please check **www.PacktPub.com** for information on our titles

Scala for Machine Learning

ISBN: 978-1-78355-874-2   Paperback: 520 pages

Leverage Scala and Machine Learning to construct and study systems that can learn from data

1. Explore a broad variety of data processing, machine learning, and genetic algorithms through diagrams, mathematical formulation, and source code.

2. Leverage your expertise in Scala programming to create and customize AI applications with your own scalable machine learning algorithms.

3. Experiment with different techniques, and evaluate their benefits and limitations using real-world financial applications, in a tutorial style.

Scala for Java Developers

ISBN: 978-1-78328-363-7   Paperback: 282 pages

Build reactive, scalable applications and integrate Java code with the power of Scala

1. Learn the syntax interactively to smoothly transition to Scala by reusing your Java code.

2. Leverage the full power of modern web programming by building scalable and reactive applications.

3. Easy to follow instructions and real world examples to help you integrate java code and tackle big data challenges.

Please check **www.PacktPub.com** for information on our titles